Business Guides on the Go

"Business Guides on the Go" presents cutting-edge insights from practice on particular topics within the fields of business, management, and finance. Written by practitioners and experts in a concise and accessible form the series provides professionals with a general understanding and a first practical approach to latest developments in business strategy, leadership, operations, HR management, innovation and technology management, marketing or digitalization. Students of business administration or management will also benefit from these practical guides for their future occupation/careers.

These Guides suit the needs of today's fast reader.

Arist von Schlippe • Tom A. Rüsen

Conflicts and Conflict Dynamics in Business Families

Dealing with Internal Family Disputes

Arist von Schlippe
Witten Institute for Family Business
Witten/Herdecke University
Witten, Germany

Tom A. Rüsen
Witten Institute for Family Business
Witten/Herdecke University
Witten, Germany

ISSN 2731-4758   ISSN 2731-4766 (electronic)
Business Guides on the Go
ISBN 978-3-031-50225-5   ISBN 978-3-031-50226-2 (Ebook)
https://doi.org/10.1007/978-3-031-50226-2

Translated, revised and expanded version of the German-language edition: Konflikte und Konfliktdynamiken in Unternehmerfamilien, by Arist von Schlippe, Tom A. Rüsen Copyright ©2020 WIFU Stiftung.

© The Editor(s) (if applicable) and The Author(s), under exclusive license to Springer Nature Switzerland AG 2024
All illustrations © Björn v. Schlippe 2023. All Rights Reserved.

This work is subject to copyright. All rights are solely and exclusively licensed by the Publisher, whether the whole or part of the material is concerned, specifically the rights of reprinting, reuse of illustrations, recitation, broadcasting, reproduction on microfilms or in any other physical way, and transmission or information storage and retrieval, electronic adaptation, computer software, or by similar or dissimilar methodology now known or hereafter developed.
The use of general descriptive names, registered names, trademarks, service marks, etc. in this publication does not imply, even in the absence of a specific statement, that such names are exempt from the relevant protective laws and regulations and therefore free for general use.
The publisher, the authors, and the editors are safe to assume that the advice and information in this book are believed to be true and accurate at the date of publication. Neither the publisher nor the authors or the editors give a warranty, expressed or implied, with respect to the material contained herein or for any errors or omissions that may have been made. The publisher remains neutral with regard to jurisdictional claims in published maps and institutional affiliations.

This Springer imprint is published by the registered company Springer Nature Switzerland AG
The registered company address is: Gewerbestrasse 11, 6330 Cham, Switzerland

Paper in this product is recyclable

Foreword: No Time to Lose

Conflict, a constant companion of human interaction since the dawn of time, is no stranger to families. Family members that are in business together are faced with an even more complex situation, as the interaction of family and business systems can spark conflict (Eddleston & Kellermanns, 2007). When relationship conflict occurs, one needs to act swiftly to mitigate its negative consequences. Family members that are intertwined in the business do not always have the opportunity to exit without high financial and/or emotional costs, a situation aptly characterised as "family wars" (Gordon & Nicholson, 2008). In these high relationship conflict situations, as in war, such costs are high for each party. Accordingly, it is paramount to understand how conflicts emerge, to understand one's own role in these conflicts, and to prevent or at the very least manage the conflict successfully after its inception.

Surprisingly, the research on conflict management is relatively sparse (for a recent review, see Qui & Freel, 2020). Family firm literature (that written in English) has mostly focused on the outcomes of conflict and its antecedents. To resolve this imbalance, the book *Conflicts and Conflict Dynamics in Business Families: Dealing with Internal Family Disputes* introduces the insights of two German authors to both the English-speaking academia and business families. I have been privileged to know both authors very well and have worked with Arist v. Schlippe on a few projects. Therefore, I can attest that the work the authors have done has and continues to provide help and guidance to countless business families in Germany. The authors' depth of knowledge that is now conveyed in this book, previously available almost exclusively to a German-speaking audience, is presented in a very engaging way, augmented with relevant examples and amusing illustrations.

I hope that the information and advice provided here will not only spark additional research in the academic community but will also lay out the path for many business families to prevent conflict dynamics and to avoid conflict escalation. There is no time to lose!

Reese Chair, UNC Charlotte Franz Kellermanns
Charlotte, NC, USA

References

Eddleston, K., & Kellermanns, F. W. (2007). Destructive and productive family relationships: A stewardship theory perspective. *Journal of Business Venturing, 22*(4), 545–565.

Gordon, G., & Nicholson, N. (2008). *Family wars. Classic conflicts in family business and how to deal with them*. Kogan Page.

Qui, H., & Freel, M. (2020). Managing family-related conflicts in family businesses: A review and reserach agenda. *Family Business Review, 33*(1), 90–113.

Preface

In family businesses, it is often conflicts within the ownership circle—the "family of the family business"—that lead to crises that potentially threaten the existence of the whole business.[1] Furthermore, businesses with a conflict-ridden owning family have considerably weakened crisis resilience. In over 20 years of working with business families at the Witten Institute for Family Business (WIFU), we have rarely seen a case in which the owners found themselves in a crisis situation solely as a result of external factors.[2] Rather, massive escalations of conflict among those involved were caused by decisions not being made, having to be revised, or not keeping pace with the demands of the market and the competition.

Of course, we are not talking of "normal" conflicts here: disagreements about tasks ("what should be done?") and processes ("how should it be done?") are important in the progress of any business.[3] However, in families, there is a higher likelihood that these conflicts will become "relationship conflicts" that jeopardise the links between and closeness of the family members. The result is, in the "best" case, individual shareholders' diminishing identification with—and withdrawal from—the owners'

---

[1] See Kellermanns and Eddlestone (2004), Gordon and Nicholson (2008), Grossmann and von Schlippe (2015), and Rüsen (2016).
[2] The COVID-19 crisis and the corporate crises of 2008–2009 resulting from the collapse of the financial system are exceptions in this respect.
[3] Eddleston and Kellermanns (2004, 2007).

association. However, this is frequently associated with a substantial capital outflow from the company, and a lack of financial resources can precipitate a strategic company crisis if important acquisitions or investments can no longer be made or are delayed. Given what we know about the decisive role of the family in a family business,[4] the risk is high that severe relationship conflict within the family will endanger the company.

Such conflicts also reduce the likelihood of constructive follow-up communication between family members, and even more crucially between generations. Once caught up in conflict communication, it is very difficult for business families without the appropriate knowledge or external support to extricate themselves. Even in the absence of escalating "family wars" (the worst-case scenario), relationship conflicts may turn into "cold conflicts", leading to a reduction in contact and communication and, ultimately, a loss of any intergenerational sense of community. Instead of seeing themselves as trustees committed to preserving the joint family business, individuals now tend to prioritise their personal wishes and goals. Unresolved conflict in the family may, thus, be the beginning of the end of the transgenerational family project. The personal injuries, emotional burdens, and psychological and physical costs for business family members, resulting from unresolved family conflict, are significant and may even lead to serious emotional stress and mental illness.[5]

Taking into account the important and dramatic consequences that family conflicts can have for the survival of a family business—and the quality of life of the family members—it is surprising that the topic of *conflict prevention* in business families has been given relatively little importance to date.[6] Business families often hide behind the fiction that they will, in the end, reach an agreement as a family. Family conflicts then leave those involved even less protected and bring resolvable issues to escalate into unbridgeable differences, to the point where family members break off their relationship or leave the community.

---

[4] Bertrand and Schoar (2006).
[5] For example, Simon (2008), Tucker et al. (2017), and Rüsen and Hörsting (2022).
[6] See in detail Rüsen and Löhde (2021).

We are convinced that conflict resolution competence is, therefore, a fundamental skill needed by every shareholder, just as important as the ability to read a balance sheet, profit and loss statement, or annual report. In this context, the need to acquire a knowledge of the specific conflict dynamics in family businesses is comparable to completing a first aid course before being qualified to drive a motor vehicle.

Business families who want to live up to the values created by previous generations, who have responsibility for their employees and also the assets of their descendants, need to familiarise themselves with the basic logic of conflicts, their typical course, the patterns they follow, and how to interrupt these patterns. This forms the basis of effective conflict prevention. Ideally, this strategy will be developed and continually updated as part of the business family's strategic development process. If business families can create a constructive view of conflict and see it as inherent in interactions within those families—as a natural part of them—the opportunities for change that lie in conflict will become clearer. Business families who succeed in removing the taboo from conflict are able to use it in a targeted way to create systematic development opportunities for the family community after the conflict has been resolved.

To this end, a "conflict-friendly" attitude is needed. We hope that the contents of this practical guide—which summarise more than one and a half decades of joint experience from a multitude of research projects, conflict management, and family strategy counselling projects—will contribute to this. Alongside the business families concerned, we have both learned a great deal from these conflicts, and they have brought us closer in both our professional collaboration and our private friendship. May this guide be similarly successful for the readers and the business families who benefit from it.

Witten, Germany Arist von Schlippe
Witten, Germany Tom A. Rüsen
November 2023

References

Bertrand, M., & Schoar, A. (2006). The role of family in family firms. *Journal of Economic Perspectives, 20*(2), S. 73–96

Eddleston, K., & Kellermanns, F. (2007). Destructive and productive family relationships: A stewardship theory perspective. *Journal of Business Venturing, 22*(4), 545–565.

Gordon, G., & Nicholson, N. (2008). *Family wars: Classic conflicts in family business and how to deal with them*. Kogan.

Grossmann, St., & von Schlippe, A. (2015). Conflict in family businesses – Family businesses: Fertile environments for conflict. *Journal of Family Business Management, 5*(2), 294–314.

Kellermanns, F. W., & Eddleston, K. A. (2004). Feuding families: When conflict does a family firm good. *Entrepreneurship Theory and Practice, 28*(3), 209–228.

Rüsen, T. A. (2016). *Krisen und Krisenmanagement in Familienunternehmen* (2. Aufl.). Springer.

Rüsen, T. A., & Hörsting, A.-K. (2022). Den psychischen Belastungen in einer Unternehmerfamilie als duales Beraterteam begegnen. *Familiendynamik, 47*(2), 142–146.

Rüsen, T. A., & Löhde, A. S. (2021). *The Business Family and its Family Strategy – Insights into the lived Practice of Family Governance*. Study of the Witten Institute for Family Business (WIFU). WIFU.

Simon, F. B. (2008). Familienunternehmen als Risikofaktor. In von A. Schlippe, A. Nischak, & M. El Hachimi (Eds.), *Familienunternehmen verstehen. Gründer, Gesellschafter, Generationen* (pp. 55–64). Vandenhoeck & Ruprecht.

Tucker, R., Shanine, K., & Combs, J. (2017). The Janus-effect: Psychopathy in family business. In F. W. Kellermanns, & F. Hoy (Eds.), *The Routledge Companion to Family Business* (pp. 459–480). Routledge.

Contents

1 **Conflict in Business Families: The Need for Family Governance** 1
   References 8

2 **An "Impossible" Connection** 11
   2.1 Family, Business, Ownership: Three Different Systems, Three Different Logics 12
   2.2 Paradoxes 20
   2.3 "The Paradox of Justice" and "Emotional Messiness" in the Business Family 23
   2.4 The "Duplicated" Family 28
   2.5 So, Why Not Say: "Family and Business Don't Work Together!" 30
   2.6 Conclusion: The Business Family as an "Emotional Arena" 31
   References 33

3 **Typical Conflict: Courses and Mechanisms** 35
   3.1 Attributing the Cause to a Single Person and the Insinuation of Motives 36
   3.2 Errors in Social Perception 38
   3.3 Violated Sense of Justice and Indignation 41
   3.4 Psychological Contracts 43

3.5 Momentum of Escalation: The "Parasite" — 45
3.6 Escalation Stages and the "Four Horsemen of the Apocalypse" — 48
3.7 The Transgenerational Transmission of Conflict Histories — 52
3.8 Threatened Sense of Belonging — 53
References — 54

4 Dealing with Conflicts on the Individual Level: Unfollow the Prescribed Patterns — 57
4.1 Individual Work: Reflecting on One's Own Part — 57
4.2 Distinction: Interests and Positions — 58
4.3 Breaking Out of the Vicious Cycle I: Slow Down — 60
4.4 Breaking Out of the Vicious Circle II: Gestures, the Magic Word "Partially", and "Small Credit Offers" — 60
4.5 Breaking Out of the Vicious Cycle III: Make Yourself Unpredictable — 62
4.6 Breaking Out of the Vicious Circle IV: Assuming Good Intentions — 65
References — 65

5 Dealing with Conflicts on the Collective Level: Family Strategy and More — 67
5.1 Classification of the Conflict and the Solution Level — 67
5.2 Conflict Prevention Within Family Strategy Development — 69
5.3 (Ideal) Five-Stage Procedure for Managing Conflicts — 73
5.4 Last but Not Least: Reflective Questions on Building Conflict Skills and Conflict Management Competence Within the Business Family — 75
References — 76

6 Wrap-Up: 18 Key Phrases — 79

Responsible for the Content — 81

About the Authors

Arist von Schlippe is Chair in "Leadership and Dynamics in Family Business" in the "Witten Institute for Family Business" (WIFU) at the Faculty of Management and Economics, Witten/Herdecke University, Germany, graduate and PhD in psychology, specialising in family therapy and family psychology, postdoctoral lecture qualification (habilitation) in clinical psychology and psychotherapy, licensed psychological psychotherapist, and licensed teacher for systemic therapy, counselling, and supervision (SG, Berlin) and has numerous national and international publications on systemic family therapy and family businesses.
Homepage: www.wifu.de

Tom A. Rüsen is CEO of the non-profit WIFU Foundation and managing director of the Witten Institute for Family Business (WIFU). He is a honorary professor of the economics faculty of the Witten/Herdecke University and a visiting professor at the Lucerne University of Applied Sciences and Arts. His research, teaching activities, and publications focus on the investigation of conflict and crisis dynamics in families and companies of family businesses and the development of practical solution concepts. As part of his coaching and consulting work, he accompanies succession processes, conflict and crisis situations, and the development of family strategies and family-internal (self-) management systems. He has numerous national and international publications on family business topics.
Web: www.wifu.de

1

Conflict in Business Families: The Need for Family Governance

Conflicts are subliminally inherent in families as well as in organisations. How much would some family members like to fall with their heads into the bowl of soup on the appropriate family occasion to cause a stir, how much would they like to publicly expose their superiors—and it doesn't happen because they themselves have an interest in maintaining this system. Except for those tipping moments when this falls apart.[1]

> **Key Phrase:**
> Family businesses are fertile fields for conflict.[2]

Conflict is an inevitable part of life. It is certainly no coincidence that a story of fatal family conflict occurs in the Bible shortly after the Creation and Expulsion from Paradise—a conflict which ends in the death of one of the brothers, Abel, while turning the other, Cain, into a murderer. The

---

[1] Wetzel and Dievernich (2014).
[2] Harvey and Evans (1994), Grossmann and von Schlippe (2015).

ancient scripture presents the theme of conflict as a normal occurrence on the one hand: disputes even occurred in the very first family! The message is, therefore, that conflict is a fundamental social phenomenon, but there is on the other hand also a warning: conflicts develop their own dynamic; they can quickly escalate and become so powerful that those involved are tempted to do terrible things. Conflicts, therefore, have to be accepted as a part of everyday human life, and learning to deal with them is one of the most important aspects of the development and socialisation of every human being.

The opportunity to say "no" is part of the human condition and determines human development. Without conflict, there will be no development and no dynamics. Often, such conflicts take place in the social—that is mainly, the family—environment. For many people, the family is still where we live most closely with others and, thus, where the ability to deal with conflict is learned. To this day, despite considerable scepticism, the lifelong mutual bond between family members is considered the most fundamental form of social life, regardless of whether the parents cohabit or are married, whether the children are biological or adopted, whether the family is nuclear, blended, or "bi-nuclear" (with children living alternately with the separated partners). The literature on the family and the psychology of the family is so extensive as to be almost unmanageable[3]—and much has also been written about family conflicts in general.[4] Therefore, the question of why we are providing a guide to dealing with conflicts in business families (and thus, of course, also in family businesses) deserves an answer.

The essential reason is that business families are very special families—their dynamics differ in many ways from those of other families. If special qualities are attributed to the family business because the family exerts a significant influence on the business, it may be assumed by implication that families and family members are also shaped in a particular way by their business. In both cases, there is a unique connection between two social systems which could hardly be more different. Owning a joint business, which becomes a major focus in the family's constant

---

[3] Liddle et al. (2006).
[4] Koerner and Fitzpatrick (2006).

communication, has an enormous impact on the family—just as family ownership has a significant effect on the business.

In our text, we will focus on conflicts in the business family.[5] For the family members, the business is, first of all, a source of wealth and happiness. This is exactly what had driven the founder to establish the business and to decide, at some point, that the business should also enable future generations to live as carefree a life as possible. However, with this transgenerational gift comes a challenge for the business family, namely, that of being an asset to the company and, above all, remaining capable of making decisions. It is indeed a challenge: managing a business or group—often of substantial financial value—and its operations does not happen by itself. Therefore, alongside the governance of the company, there is a need for *family governance*.[6] In contrast to other families, business families have a "big issue" which takes a central position in family communication—alongside the many everyday family burdens—and this does not necessarily make it easier to handle potential conflict. It is not, therefore, surprising that the gossip press and specialist literature are full of stories in which the business also leads to stress, quarrels, and unhappiness for the family (and vice versa). The consequences here can be dramatic: "The greatest value destroyer in the family business is strife."[7]

In order to understand conflict in the context of family businesses, we need to know more about conflict dynamics. Going one step further,

---

[5] The framework of this guide offers only limited scope to address the complex topic of "conflicts". For an in-depth understanding of conflicts in business families, we recommend von Schlippe and Frank (2017), and Chapter 10 in Zellweger's book *Managing the Family Business* (2017); the books *It can Happen in the Best of Families* and *The Carousel of Indignation and Outrage* (von Schlippe, 2014, 2022b) are only available in German. You may find significant information on the website of John Davis: https://cfeg.com/insights_research/understanding-conflict-in-the-family-business/ or on the pages of the Family Enterprise Foundation: https://familyenterprisefoundation.org/learning-community/understand-with-courses/communication-and-conflict-management-for-business-families/. In addition, we recommend the video recordings of lectures by the authors on the topic of conflict dynamics and conflict prevention posted on the WIFU homepage as well as the WIFU practical guide *Conflict Management in Family Businesses* by Daniel Otte (download at www.wifu.de)

[6] On this topic, see the WIFU practical guide *Family strategy development in business families—content and forms of family governance and family management systems* by Rüsen, von Schlippe, & Groth (2022) (download at www.wifu.de). See also von Schlippe et al. (2021).

[7] Hennerkes and Kirchdörfer (2015), p. 62, Translated by the authors (like all following citations) from German sources.

however, it makes sense to think about what is so special about business families. What effect does the business have on the communication structures in the family? What does it expect of the individual members? How do they manage the significant increase in complexity that results from this special configuration?

These are precisely the issues that we will address: we will briefly outline the particular challenges faced by business families and follow this with a description of the possible conflict situations in which these families can become involved and the options available to counter them—either proactively or preventatively through a clever family strategy or family governance or, if "the horse has already bolted", to manage them in a way that heads towards a solution rather than aggravating them.

Conflicts are not inevitable for business families, but their probability is certainly high because, when it comes to central life issues of a private, personal, and professional nature, emotions can quickly run high. After all, there is a great deal at stake:

- The family members' identity is often closely linked to their name and the company.[8] Closely related to this are emotional questions about the essential human need to belong[9]—here seen as membership and the individual's "place" in the system. Company logic and family logic address membership in entirely different ways: while a person can easily cease to belong to a firm, family membership cannot be "terminated" as such. Exclusion from a position in the family business, therefore, can certainly be extremely hurtful from the family logic perspective. Anything that affects the family company quickly leads to personal involvement.
- The topics generally at the centre of conflicts are of high psychological importance—a whole life's work (for the senior generation) or the core values of those involved: love (and jealousy of the company), loyalty, commitment, and significant sacrifice, often on the part of spouses or children. If these are not recognised and valued by the other side to the

---

[8] Emotional ownership; see Björnberg and Nicholson (2012).
[9] See Baumeister and Leary (1995).

extent it is felt they should be, feelings of grievance and rejection can grow quickly. Unfortunately, when these are communicated in the form of reproaches and accusations, the likelihood of achieving the desired outcome is usually reduced. Lastly, but equally importantly, typical issues of sibling competition and jealousy are, within the context of the family business, quickly magnified.

> **Case Example: The Patriarch's Daughter**
>
> A woman had, with some reluctance, accepted the fact that her father, on his deathbed, had chosen to appoint her elder sister to run the family business, and not herself. She had chosen to study economics (as had her sister) with the specific aim of taking over from her father, working alongside her sister for years as part of the management team and dedicating time and effort to the company during the tough post-war years and beyond. Her husband was also involved in the early post-war years and had secured a large-scale, long-term contract at that difficult time which had ensured the company's lasting stability. Even after her father's death, she continued to work for the company now as a subordinate of her sister. However, at the company's 100th-anniversary celebration, her sister made no mention of her or her husband at all: "She started talking of our father as the founder, and then all she said was: 'I did this, I did that!'" The younger sister was so deeply hurt that the relationship between the siblings broke down entirely. All that it would have taken was for the elder sister to mention her sister appreciatively, highlighting the part that she and her husband had played in the history of the company and expressing her gratitude—five or ten minutes in the whole speech would have made all the difference.

- Jealousy and social comparison can play an important role, especially between siblings: The "theory of social comparison" was developed in the 1950s and is concerned with how an individual's self-esteem frequently depends on how they perceive and describe themselves in relation to those close to them: Do others love me more or less? (oh dear—it is so easy to become insecure about that one)? Do I have more or less money/assets than that other person—regardless of whether what I have is more than sufficient to last a lifetime? Am I regarded by others as being more or less important, as meaningful? Do I count? These profound psychological issues are significant in most families, and all siblings observe each other carefully in terms of parental relations: this is why symbolic acts are so important. "You didn't have time to come to my birthday party but you came all the way from France, especially for my sister's!" In business families, there is an added factor here: a son who has perhaps been chosen early on as the potential successor is more likely to be taken into the business by the father, and the intimate relationship that will develop between the two that is observed jealously by the other siblings, especially the sisters. Thus, family members observe the distribution of non-material resources (love, recognition, protection), each keeping a personal account of the benefits or deficits against their name, comparing them with those of the others.[10] However, this "account-keeping" is only evident at certain points in time. Especially when inheritance is involved, the "fictional consensus" according to which families may have lived together in apparent contentment for many years gets lost, and unpleasant surprises may occur, resulting in dramatic conflict dynamics. When the "balance sheets" are presented, it may finally become clear how great the differences are: decisions then have to be made about who gets the house, the ring, the picture ("Why should it be her, or him, and not me?").

- Closely related to jealousy are questions regarding perceived fairness. These are crucial in all close human relationships. The need for fairness is apparently universal: people react extremely to perceived injustice inflicted on themselves or on others, and the *belief in a just world* is actively upheld and not questioned, although it may be considered a "fundamental delusion".[11] People all over the world seem to agree in demanding justice, which is regarded as a central motif in all cultures, especially in close relationships: "Perceived injustices are at the core of everyday conflicts in private life".[12]
- However—and here lies the problem—there are huge differences between what is described as fair and what is felt to be so. The contradiction between what is sensed as fair and the logic of fairness creates a constant source of tension—in the family context and others. This is

---

[10] Boszormenyi-Nagy and Spark (1973).
[11] Lerner (1980).
[12] Montada (2003, p. 538). We will return to the issue of justice later.

due to the fact that everybody keeps tabs on their own personal "fairness balance sheet" which indicates where they stand in relation to the most important people in their immediate social environment. The degree of perceived unfairness can be measured by the level of indignation and outrage[13]: "After everything I've done for the family/the business/my father—and now this!" Indeed, an injured sense of justice and the outrage that arises from it are probably the foundation of all conflict (see Chap. 3).

- An additional aspect fuels conflicts in business families in particular: the many third parties who become drawn into the complex processes. Since considerable material assets are at stake, external professionals are involved, including tax advisers, accountants, and lawyers. The business family is often observed very closely by external managers since, as far as they are concerned, much depends on family relations remaining stable (if not, intrafamilial differences may in danger to be used in "micropolitics" by externals). If the business is faced with potential difficulties, coaches, consultancy firms, and their staff may also be involved. All these outsiders not only observe the business activities but also form their own perspective of the family itself and how it relates to the business and, of course, will happily offer their own observations: "No, there is no way you can hand over the company to your daughter, she is surely not capable of taking it on." In such cases, it is not always clear whether it is solely the interests of the company that are being protected or whether such individuals are in fact pursuing their own interests.
- Another important issue is caused by the strong bonds created by the joint business and the joint assets. This can make it more difficult to leave the parental family in young adulthood and form a new family of one's own. In business families, the parental family often has stronger bonds than in other families, making the process of detachment harder. Let us just imagine one of those scenes in which some crisis requires the junior boss to be in the office on Sunday, while their spouse and children have to go to the zoo alone—"Again!" (sometimes these little

---

[13] von Schlippe (2022a).

incidents pile up to become a significant source of marital or family discontent).
- Finally, it is also about money. Money has a strong binding force, and often not in a positive sense.[14] Moreover, it makes it more difficult to solve a problem by just walking away. The option to regulate the conflict by distancing oneself is not as readily available as it might be to other families. Even if a family member decides to cancel contact, not wanting anything more to do with the family, a few weeks later the postman will deliver the invitation to the shareholders' meeting—at which their own assets are at stake. The costs of not attending might be very high; thus, the "grip" of the parental family is felt through money and people rarely choose freedom over money (—some do!).

All these issues seep into communication. Expressed with varying degrees of agitation, anger, insult, or bitterness, they may lead to vicious circles of mutual misunderstanding and deepen the sense of being attacked or treated unfairly often on both sides—with corresponding reactions. In a downward spiral, the likelihood of conflict escalation is further increased. Generally, then, business families have an emotional and communicative mix that is more conducive to conflict than other families. It is a minefield that, for years, might be navigated successfully until, at some point, someone accidentally steps on a "hidden mine" and the conflict explodes.

Let us take a closer look at why it is that these affective states can be found in conflict in general and particularly in business families.

References

Baumeister, R. F., & Leary, M. R. (1995). The need to belong: Desire for interpersonal attachments as a fundamental human motivation. *Psychological Bulletin, 117*(3), 497–529.

---

[14] Blouin and Gibson (1995).

Björnberg, A., & Nicholson, N. (2012). Emotional ownership: The next generation's relationship with the family firm. *Family Business Review, 25*(4), 374–390.
Blouin, B., & Gibson, K. (1995). *The legacy of inherited wealth*. Trio Press.
Boszormenyi-Nagy, I., & Spark, G. (1973). *Invisible loyalties. Reciprocity in intergenerational family therapy*. Harper & Row.
Grossmann, S., & von Schlippe, A. (2015). Conflict in family businesses – Family businesses: Fertile environments for conflict. *Journal of Family Business Management, 5*(2), 294–314.
Harvey, M., & Evans, R. E. (1994). Family business and multiple levels of conflict. *Family Business Review, 7*(4), 331–348.
Hennerkes, B.-H., & Kirchdörfer, R. (2015). *Die Familie und ihr Unternehmen. Strategie, Liquidität, Kontrolle*. Campus.
Koerner, A. F., & Fitzpatrick, M. A. (2006). Family conflict communication. In J. Oetzel & S. Ting-Toomey (Eds.), *The Sage handbook of conflict communication: Integrating theory, research, and practice* (pp. 159–183). Sage.
Lerner, M. J. (1980). *The belief in a just world: A fundamental delusion*. Plenum Press.
Liddle, H., Santisteban, D., Levant, R., & Bray, J. (Eds.). (2006). *Family psychology. Science-based interventions*. APA.
Montada, L. (2003). Justice, equity and fairness. In J. Weiner (Ed.), *Handbook of psychology* (Vol. 5, pp. 537–568). Wiley.
Rüsen, T. A., von Schlippe, A., & Groth, T. (2022). *Family strategy development in business families – Content and forms of family governance and family management systems*. Practical guide of the Witten Institute for Family Business (WIFU). WIFU.
von Schlippe, A. (2014). *Das kommt in den besten Familien vor. Systemische Konfliktberatung in Familien und Familienunternehmen* (1. Aufl.). Concadora.
von Schlippe, A. (2022a). *Das Karussell der Empörung. Eskalierte Konflikte verstehen und begrenzen*. Vandenhoeck & Ruprecht.
von Schlippe, A. (2022b). Family businesses in coaching: Specific dynamics. In S. Greif, H. Möller, W. Scholl, J. Passmore, & F. Müller (Eds.), *International handbook of evidence-based coaching* (pp. 325–336). Springer.
von Schlippe, A., & Frank, H. (2017). Conflict in family business in the light of systems theory. In F. Kellermanns & F. Hoy (Eds.), *The Routledge companion to family business* (pp. 367–384). Routledge.
von Schlippe, A., Rüsen, T., & Groth, T. (2021). *The two sides of the business family. Governance and strategy across generations*. Springer.

Wetzel, R., & Dievernich, F. (2014). Der Gott des Gemetzels. Wie Organisationen und Familien auf modernen Gleichheitsdruck reagieren. *Kontext*, *45*(2), 126–154.

Zellweger, T. (2017). *Managing the family business. Theory and practice*. Edward Elgar.

2

An "Impossible" Connection

Key Phrase:
Conflict in business families should be seen as "the rule"; rather, the absence of conflict should be regarded as the exception that needs explanation.

Definition
For the purpose of this text, family businesses are understood to be businesses that are wholly or partly owned by the family, regardless of the size of their share of the business.[1] At the same time, the family exerts a discernible influence on the development of the business, whether through executive functions or supervisory bodies such as advisory boards, family councils, supervisory boards, or similar. "The business family (however ramified it may have become over the course of its history) has the overall entrepreneurial responsibility for the business (regardless of how able or unable it is to bear this responsibility)".[2] Another necessary characteristic is the transgenera-

---

[1] Chua et al. (1999).
[2] Wimmer (2014, p. 27).

> tional aspect: several generations are visibly involved—even if this is simply at the planning stage, for example in a company still managed by the founder whose intention it is to hand over some day to the next generation.

2.1 Family, Business, Ownership: Three Different Systems, Three Different Logics

The members of a business family find themselves constantly balancing their membership in and the communication logics of three different social systems: as family members, as either part of the business (executives or board members) or affected by the business communication, and as owners (or future owners, partners etc.) affected by the communication logic of the ownership system.[3] The three systems all bring different issues.[4]

- *Family Logic: Relationship communication*
- The *family* is a system "built" around love, attachment, relationships and loyalty: gestures of affection are exchanged (to a greater or lesser extent); people are mutually supportive and personal dedication is rewarded with gratitude and appreciation. This specific family function is commonly referred to as relationship-, connection- or attachment-communication. The family logic of balancing inequalities between members generally concerns gratitude rather than monetary rewards, and the compensation is usually not expected immediately or "at the end of the month" (as in a company) but perhaps years later (for instance at family gatherings), or sometimes even after generations ("I want you to have a better life"). A single mother who has been working for years to enable her daughter to go to university will not demand $250,000 "in cash, please" when the daughter qualifies as a doctor, but she will expect gratitude, recognition and appreciation.

---

[3] The classic "three circles" system was introduced by Tagiuri and Davis (1996).
[4] For example, von Schlippe and Frank (2013).

Communication is, therefore, focused on attachment and bonding, and any decision is double-checked as regards what it may mean for the relationship.
- *Company Logic: Decision Communication*
- In contrast, the *business* as a social system does not put relationships first (otherwise it would e.g. be impossible to dismiss anybody). Whereas in the family it's always *the whole person* who is of interest, in the company only a *part of the person* is considered significant, namely that part which fulfils the particular function for which the person has been employed. Thus, companies are social systems "built" around "decision communication"[5] (Luhmann, 2000): Any communication will be checked for what it might mean for the core job of the business: decision-making. While a complaint about a headache in the family will usually lead to a sympathetic and caring response, in the company that person will hear a short "I'm sorry" followed by "But - does that mean you can't work today?" The communication logic is functional in nature: each individual's capabilities are observed and put to use, while compensation is oriented to the short term, and remuneration in the form of a salary settles all reciprocal claims.
- *Owner's Logic: Legal and financial communication*
- Among business owners, *ownership* and shares in the business are the pivotal "currency". Owning a share gives certain legal rights; as long as these are granted, the ownership systems function effectively, and individuals will be recompensed with dividends and reputation.

A problem in family businesses, however, is the permanent mingling of family, organisational, and ownership communication because the contexts are not clearly distinguishable. In everyday life, so-called "context markers" will help clarify which logic applies to which context (the signs "restaurant", "station", and "university" all indicate different communication logics at work, as do specific clothing, uniforms, etc.). At home, communication clearly follows a logic of intimacy and familiarity. In

---

[5] Luhmann (2000).

business families, however, there are no clear markers to indicate how a communicative offer is to be understood. It frequently is not easy to define the context unmistakably as "family" or "work". Communication logics may shift and blur into one another (and the actors concerned are usually not aware of the mingling).

> - For example, a husband and wife, both managers in the family business, continually found themselves engaged in intense debate about the strategic reorientation of the company over breakfast, and in the bedroom too—even this room did not clearly signal "Only personal communication here".
> - In another family, the founding father, now chair of the board, and his CEO daughter were attending a board meeting when the father took out his glasses, looked at them, and passed them to her: "Just clean those, dear!" Even the context of the board meeting did not prevent habitual forms of family communication between father and daughter from breaking into the business context, even though at that moment they were there as CEO and chair of the board—different "persons" in a non-family situation.
> - In a third example, two brothers were in conflict (one the CEO and the other the holder of the other half of the shares but with no position in the firm). The CEO said to his brother, "Why aren't you just grateful that I've multiplied the value of the business ten-fold through my hard work over the last 25 years—and you've benefited by receiving all the dividends!" (note the family communication logic here, demanding gratitude). The brother answered, in organisational logic, "So what! You've always been paid your salary, haven't you? And another manager might have even done better!"

The list could be easily extended. Such inconsistencies between the logic of the family and that of the business are reported again and again by business families, and strategy debates at the breakfast table are a relatively harmless example. It is more difficult when misunderstandings arise when one person communicates using one logic while the other person is using another. This is what we mean by "skewed connections": one communication connects to the other in the context of a different system.

We can distinguish between the behavioural expectations in a family, a company, or a group of shareholders who manage a common ownership.

The family, business, and ownership are three systems, each with its own specific logic. As long as the contexts are neatly separated, the conflicts between the different systems are manageable: the expectations of how to communicate in the social systems of work and family differ, and by opening the office door we automatically enter a different logic system. In family businesses and business families, however, the boundaries between the contexts can become blurred, and it may become difficult to identify which context a communication belongs to.

Let us take an even closer look at the logics: communication in the family focuses on attachments and relationships. Everything that happens in the family is considered from the perspective of what it means for these relationships. The logic of the business, on the other hand, is based on the need to make decisions. Anything that does not lead directly—or at least indirectly—to a decision does not, strictly speaking, belong to the organisation.

The contexts of family and business are generally easy to distinguish in everyday life: we leave home in the morning and go to work. One logic applies in one context and another in the other. However, this is where things become difficult in business families, because for them the family logic and business logic are not that easily distinguishable—they flow smoothly into each other. Which logic governs the communication when strategy is discussed at breakfast, or when a decision is discussed in the living room in the evening? Let us imagine that the manager of the family business says to their son or daughter, "Oh, by the way, I've decided to assign the project management to Mr. Meier" and is met with the disappointed comment, "You've never trusted me with anything." The reader can probably already see the issue: a communication in the business logic is met by relationship logic here; the difference of the logics creates a sophisticated kind of misunderstanding, not related to the logic of the words spoken but to the wider context of family and business. These types of interaction are known as "skewed" or "weird connections" and they can explain some of the conflict dynamics in business families.[6]

---

[6] See Leaptrott (2005).

Weird Connections

The following example shows just such a situation—a conflict between a father and son that almost broke up a family.[7]

A business family, let us call them the Abel family, asked for advice. In the course of planning the succession, the family members had fallen out to such an extent that they could no longer manage the conflicts in which they had become entangled. From the first conversations, a highly aggressive tension was palpable and now, as soon as the first words were spoken, the conversation plunged into difficult waters. Strong feelings of dismay and grievance were evident among the participants, alongside a firm conviction on the part of each that the other person was the sole source of their own unhappiness and, thus, the anger and indignation they felt.

The conflict presented the counsellors with a series of puzzles from the start: Why were they so extremely angry with each other, despite—or perhaps on account of—clearly liking one another very much (they had arrived from different places and greeted each other very warmly) and an absence, apart from a few heated exchanges, of any hostility. Both sides were clearly willing to cooperate; why, then, was it not possible to achieve this? And what had it all to do with the succession?

Obviously, it was connected in some way to this issue because, as the family reported, the possibility of reasonably calm conversation had stopped shortly after the parents had offered their son the business succession. Through this action, a different logic had entered the family communication system. The counsellors' work with the family continued for several months to clarify the differences between family and company communication: roles were clarified, agreements made (and broken again), and relationships improved slightly for a while; then there would be another contentious incident and a return to the old pattern.

All the time, two words repeatedly came up which, it transpired, related to two key stories and proved crucial in understanding the conflict. "*Christmas*" was one word: during the Christmas holidays, the parents had offered their son and his partner the chance to succeed them as

---

[7] Abridged from von Schlippe (2014, pp. 40 f).

managers of the hotel they had built up from the grandfather's inn. Mr. and Mrs. Abel had solemnly declared that they would like to pass the business—their "jewel"—on to the next generation. This had never been expressed so explicitly before. It was a highly emotional moment; everyone was happy, and the son and future daughter-in-law had joyfully agreed. The other key term that arose again and again, being connected with strong feelings, was *"business plan"*. Shortly after the emotional Christmas event, the young people had begun working on a business plan that they presented to the parents 3 weeks later, with strategic options, proposals for structural changes, and "milestones" on the way to the final handover of the business. To their astonishment, the parents—especially the father—were deeply offended, even indignant, "How dare you? What insolence! You want to push us out of the business and make yourselves at home? That's out of the question!" Asking how the parents had envisaged the handover led nowhere. Their idea that the next generation would initially work alongside them in the business and that the details would work out was robustly rejected by the younger generation. "Oh, you're looking for cheap interns who will clean the toilets and work for you for years? You'll keep control of everything and, years later, sometime, maybe, you'll be ready to hand over? No, not with us!" It was a classic, contentious, and very hardened succession impasse: "You won't let go!" versus "You want to push us out!" Both sides were recognisably deeply affected by this escalating dispute.

In the course of discussions, it became clear that the participants—especially father and son (on whom we will focus below)—were following quite different logics in their communication. The core of the conflict could be summarised thus: In offering their "jewel" to their son, the parents were following the family logic (they even commented that "the hotel is our baby!"). The young people's response—the business plan—arose from a business logic. The communicative connections were "skewed": they did not fit the schemata expected by the respective participants, and the contexts from which each side was communicating were interpreted differently by the other. In fact, in their statements, the two parties were operating in different social systems. In a way, they were different "persons"[8] but neither was aware of this, simply seeing the same person. Neither side was aware of the paradox: they simply felt, psychologically and personally, that the other side was "wrong", "impertinent", or even "crazy".

In the first interview, one of the parents had said to one of the counsellors, "It's good that you, as a psychologist, are looking at this; you will quickly see that something is wrong with our son. We have already thought about sending him to a psychiatrist." This comment elicited an aggrieved and angry response from the son. Such descriptions are not at all uncommon in quarrelling business families. When someone communicates in a different logic, i.e. within the framework of a different system with different expectation structures, individuals quickly resort to the simplistic explanation that the other person is "stupid", "insane", or "evil" (more on this below).

In working with the Abel family, it was possible to clarify the descriptive patterns by reconstructing the "jewel and business plan" scene in a particular way. Four chairs were placed in the room, in pairs facing each other. Two of the chairs facing each other were defined as "father and son chairs". The chair next to that of the father was for the business owner; the one next to the son's chair was for the successor. The "jewel and business plan" scene was then replayed. Each person could sit on one of two chairs and this represents one of the core problems in business families. When asked which chair he had been sitting on when he offered the succession to his son, the father immediately replied that it had "of course" been the father's chair. However, the son had just as understandably been figuratively sitting on the successor's chair when the offer was made; i.e.

---

[8] In systems theory a "person" is a "communication address" (Luhmann, 1995). So, in a family context, the father is a specific *person*: the "communication address father" (and the son similarly) whereas in the context business the same human being becomes a different person, "the boss", "the successor". So, if the context markers remain unclear for both actors, it remains ambiguous as which of two "persons" one is being addressed in communication. Which person he/she "is" depends on the answer to the question, which logic is currently valid, whether the family logic or business logic is applied here. Communication may thus "get lost"; those involved may feel that something is wrong but, as they do not understand the paradox, they attribute this to the other person, unaware of the confusion of the contexts.

he had relied on business logic while listening. When they were asked to sit on the respective chairs they had used at the time, and realised they had not been sitting directly opposite each other, the cross communication became obvious. The father was asked to repeat the sentence, "We want to entrust you with our jewel". He refused, objecting "What for? There's no one sitting on that chair!" That was precisely the problem: the father had not been aware that his offer, made in the family logic, had been taken up by the son within the business logic. The son, in turn, had naturally assumed that the father had been "sitting" on the chair of the business manager at Christmas. Neither had been clear about the context of the communication and the message had, therefore, been lost. As already mentioned, this dilemma within business families can be responsible for many misunderstandings: Who is actually sitting on which "chair" internally, i.e. which logic are the interlocutors using in their communication? The constant presence of different system logics that can be experienced at the same time makes it difficult to orientate communication.

Continuing the conversation with the Abels, successful communication was finally acted out in the appropriate logics: the son sat down on the "son's chair"; the father now repeated his offer from the "father's chair" and received a touching response of gratitude from his son—experiencing this "fit" was a relief for both. He was then asked to repeat his offer from the "entrepreneur's chair". He now worded it completely differently, using business vocabulary, and the son—who had also changed chairs—responded accordingly. Suddenly, the business plan was no longer a slight, but an offer of negotiation appropriate to the context.

Figure 2.1 illustrates in a generalised manner this particular form of misunderstanding. On the right, we find successful communication: the two actors are moving within the same business logic, symbolised by the same colour clothing they are wearing. A father and son (or any other combination of sex and generation) sit opposite each other; two family members with a personal relationship, two owners negotiating the handling of assets, and two people active in the business—perhaps the

Fig. 2.1 From systemic misunderstanding to successful communication

transferor and the successor—discuss entrepreneurial issues with clear expectations of their roles. On the left, we find ambiguity and muddled communication. We can see how both are trying hard to be understood, but they are not engaging each other at all. The communication is lost because each is caught up in their own logic, as symbolised by the colour of their clothing.

2.2 Paradoxes

> **Key Phrase:**
> Many conflicts in family businesses can be understood as more or less intelligent attempts to solve paradoxical dilemmas.

The focus on the business family, as the starting point for the following considerations, reveals a very specific type of family. Unlike other families, business families are continuously faced with specific expectations from the business. As illustrated in the example of the Abel family, business families often lack clear signs of the relevant context: when does the logic of the family apply, or that of the business or ownership? The difficult situations that can arise here are often referred to as family business paradoxes.[9]

One particular form of paradox is the so-called "pragmatic paradox".[10] These come about when a paradoxical expectation is held or a paradoxical call to action is issued. "Do it but don't do it!" may not initially appear to be an instruction heard in everyday life. However, there are in fact numerous examples. They constitute the well-known phenomenon of the "double bind"—the contradiction between what communication demands and the fact that it demands it. We'll make it simpler. Take the paradox in the photographer's request to "be a bit more natural". You probably start to feel uneasy—but why? Well, two contradictory hidden requests can be found here: "Do what I tell you" and "Do something that can only be done voluntarily, without being asked." A similar situation may have well been experienced by readers: "You never say that you love me!"—"Ok, I love you!"—"But you only said it because I asked you to!"—"Well, you did, so I did!"—"Yes, but I want you to say it *voluntarily*, from your heart, not because I asked you to!"—Wise partners will wait some weeks if they want to evade this paradox…

It is, therefore, the simultaneity of contradictory behavioural expectations that define this type of paradox. Pragmatic paradoxes that occur frequently within close relationships may turn into "double binding patterns" that are associated to "mad" behaviour: someone who cannot behave "correctly", however hard they try, may act in a seemingly "mad" way to escape the paradox. They will attempt to survive in an unpredictable "universe" consisting solely of double binds—situations in which it is impossible to do the right thing[11]—by talking nonsense, for example, and thus avoiding being pinned down on one side or the other, or so Bateson and his team propose.

The paradox situation is more than a contradiction that causes a resolvable conflict. In a "double bind-constellation" two expectations are contradictory but also both essential, with the additional restriction that you

---

[9] Schuman et al. (2010), Kleve et al. (2020).
[10] Watzlawick et al. (1969).
[11] Litz (2012).

cannot simply walk away. So, you're damned if you do and damned if you don't, and you can't get away from it.[12]

Transferred to the business family, the form of the paradox—simplified again to refer only to family and business—can be understood thus (see Table 2.1):

- Expectation A: "We are a family."
- (We focus on the bonds between and relationships of our members. We make sure that no one is excluded, etc.)
- Expectation B: "We are a group of shareholders, i.e. an organisation."
- (We ensure that the business has a competent circle of owners, that the best person is chosen, that decision-making ability is guaranteed, etc.).
- At the same time, Commandment C is: "No one may leave as we need their voice as a shareholder."

Table 2.1 Differences between the logics

Type ⇒ Theme ⇓	Family system	Business system	Shareholder system
	Closely related persons of all ages	Persons who fulfil specific requirements in terms of qualifications or experience, usually not linked by family ties	Owners, in family businesses: relatives (close or distantly related)
Entry and exit: How to enter and leave?	Entry by birth, marriage, adoption. Exit in principle not possible	Entry by being offered a job, entering the company. Exit is possible at any time, depending on the contract	Entry by gaining/ inheriting property. Exit by sale
Centre of communication	Confirmation of bonding and attachment (logic of inclusion)	Company decisions (logic of selectivity)	Ownership decisions (logics of law)

---

[12] These "crazymaking conditions" were first described by Gregory Bateson; see Bateson et al. (1956).

Table 2.1 (continued)

Type ⇒	Family system	Business system	Shareholder system
Communication paths	Less formal, oral, less hierarchical	Formal, written, hierarchical	Formal, written, protocols
Making decisions	Many chances for negotiation, goal is agreement, by seniority or consensus	Little room for negotiation, hierarchical, and clarity of decision is the goal	Hierarchical, majority votes
What/who is important?	The individual (not replaceable)	Function, competence (person is replaceable if not fulfils expectations)	Number of shares, function
"Currency" exchanged	Love, attachment, loyalty	Work/effort, career, power	Shares, authority qua competence, seniority, etc.
Adequate compensation	Recognition, appreciation, gratitude, long term (possibly decades)	Salary, short term (by end of month), appreciation important, but not enforceable	Regular dividend; appreciation value
Logic of justice	Equality: Everybody gets the same (or what they need)	Inequality: Position and salary according to effort, competence	Equal in information. Not equal in voice: according to shares

Slightly modified from: von Schlippe and Frank (2017, p. 373)

2.3 "The Paradox of Justice" and "Emotional Messiness" in the Business Family

When people are unaware of the paradoxes they face, they tend to be confused; indeed, in many situations, we find that the actors feel uncertain about a decision and oscillate between options. A common paradox that many business families struggle with arises from a combination of contradictory expectations. It concerns notions of justice: Expectation

A—from the family logic—is integration—treating all the children equally. Expectation B, conversely, from the business logic, is very different: it requires the selection of the most suitable person and, if possible, the transfer of all or the majority of the shares to this person to enable them to act. These two demands—"integration" and "selectivity"—are strong and equally valid in the business family. The paradox between these logics cannot be resolved by compromise. Whatever "right" steps are taken in one direction are "wrong" in the other. Instead, a *decision* has to be made, which means there is no easy solution; either family members will feel betrayed and disappointed or the decision-making ability of the executive family members will be restricted.

In very large family businesses, these questions have been resolved long ago, and so the following generations can turn to so-called "decision premises"[13]: "That's the way we did it in our family, and so that's how we do it today". Younger, mostly smaller and medium-sized business families are more frequently affected by this paradox and its consequences. Whatever action is taken, it is "wrong" in one of the logics. Equal share distribution satisfies the family but creates decision-making problems at the company level. Different levels of shareholding ensure the managing partner's ability to act, but quickly create feelings of unfairness within the family. Even equal treatment of the children can lead to differences in the next generation. Let us look at a larger family that cannot find a solution to the justice paradox.[14]

Wilhelm, the grandfather, who is now 82 years old, is considered to be the founder; he took over a small company from his father and, over the years, expanded it so that it now has several branches and several hundred employees. The company is in good shape with no debts. Wilhelm has always felt fit but, together with his wife, Greta, who is of a similar age, he is now thinking about how to bequeath the property fairly. This is not so easy. He has a total of seven children: two from his first marriage, which lasted only 3 years, and 5 from his second marriage, which has now lasted 42 years. Most of these children have children of their own

---

[13] A term coined by Luhmann, e.g. 1995, 2000.
[14] Taken from von Schlippe (2022), translated by the authors.

and there are also five great-grandchildren between the ages of two and 11 (they are listed as fourth generation for simplicity). The grandchildren are aged between 3 and 40 years: Anton, the oldest son of the daughter from the first marriage, is older than Gert, Wilhelm's youngest son. Two sons are childless; one has an adopted child. Only one of Wilhelm's seven children (Wolfgang) is operationally active in the company (Fig. 2.2).

So far, there have been no inheritance transactions. On the advice of a lawyer, Wilhelm and Greta are now considering passing on the shares in the company—but how? Whatever solution is found, someone will feel disadvantaged and that is something families usually try to avoid at all costs. Conceivable variants include the following.

- The classic "patriarchal" solution, now fortunately considered outdated, is that only the first-born son inherits shares while the others are paid out.
- Another patriarchal solution, as outdated as the former, is to hand over the shares only to the sons and compensate the daughters.

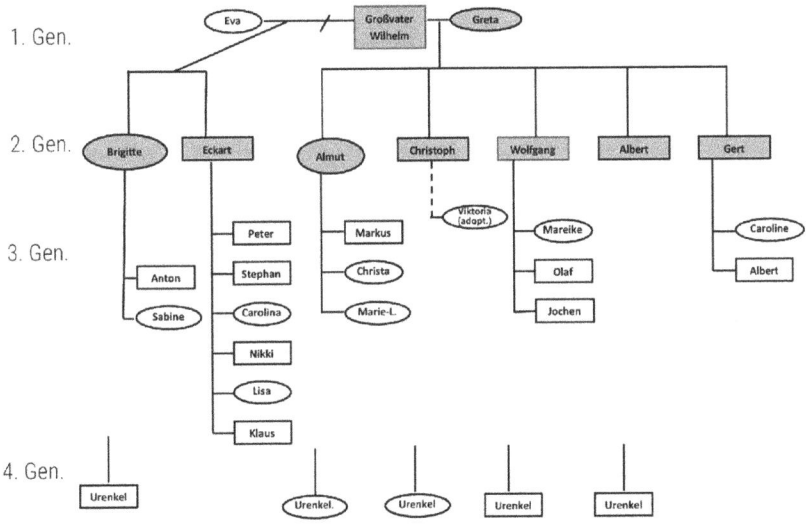

Fig. 2.2 The justice dilemma in the business family (from von Schlippe, 2022)

- In a solution that strictly follows the logic of the company, Wolfgang is the only family member who is active in the company so 100% is bequeathed to him, so that he remains able to make decisions while the others are paid out. In a similar logic, 50 or more per cent of the shares could be given to Wolfgang, with the other half distributed among the siblings.
- More in line with family logic would be to give all seven children a seventh each. However, in the next generation, what will Eckart—who would have to divide his seventh among his six children—say if the vote of his adopted niece Viktoria carries so much more weight than that of each of his children?
- In any case, wouldn't it be fair to give the two children from the first marriage a smaller share? After all, this marriage lasted only 3 years—the real marriage was the second, wasn't it? Maybe the two children from the first marriage should share one share between them and the remainder should receive a whole share each? Imagine who might complain about that solution!
- Perhaps, then, it is better to bequeath the shares to the grandchildren straight away (with the added benefit of saving inheritance tax). Each of the 17 grandchildren would now get an equal share. Then, again, there will be protest, this time from the children with fewer children of their own—Albert would go away empty-handed, while Eckart's family would suddenly bag more than one-third of the shares. Even with equal distribution to all the descendants—children, grandchildren, and great-grandchildren—the complaints would not cease.

And so on. There are many possible versions of what a "fair" division might look like, but no objectively fair solution exists. In the end, Wilhelm may therefore decide to give his company entirely to a foundation, as some entrepreneurs do.

What a dilemma. Justice is impossible, yet it is one of the core themes of human relationships,[15] and thus of course also—and especially—in families. The family is a system primarily of belonging; thus, much of

---

[15] Montada (2003).

what happens in the family is experienced existentially, with intense emotions.

Family members, however, each have their own ideas about what is just. Issues of legacy and merit are continuously scrutinised, especially in families.[16] Family members observe each other very closely against a backdrop of bonds of fidelity, demands of loyalty, and premises of justice, with offsets of merit and guilt, which can vary greatly from individual to individual. Depending on the results of such accounting, the individual feels burdened with guilt and/or shame or relieved of it. Family members have very different ideas about what one sibling is entitled to ("after all that she did for the family") or is not entitled to ("You always looked out for yourself and never cared about us, and now you come with demands? No!"). And, of course, what one sees as appropriate for oneself may be seen differently by others (we all tend to look at ourselves rather more generously).

Many questions arise in this respect:

- Who is close to whom and how? Which child is especially close to the parents? Who sees themselves as the "unloved Cinderella" or is considered a "black sheep" or outcast?
- What about the accounting of services loyally rendered by oneself, or selfishly taken advantage of by others? The care of sick parents, for example, reveals rivalry and solidarity between siblings particularly clearly: Who made a special effort for the family/parents, for example, by providing special care? And did they perhaps also take advantage of this to negotiate special conditions for themselves in the inheritance? Was this their motivation?
- Who would be seen in the debt column in the family accounting system, perhaps because they caused the parents particular grief, never bothered about the family, visited rarely or never, perhaps even tried to manipulate the parents in their favour? What if he ("of course, him again!") is sitting in the front row at the reading of the will?

---

[16] Boszormenyi-Nagy and Spark (1973).

- Who had already received special benefits during their lifetime (e.g. when buying a house, or financing further education), which, according to some, should be offset against the inheritance?

If expectations that have developed over a long period are then violated in the inheritance, feelings of profound injustice may be triggered. Here, the need for compensation can lead to strange behaviours; e.g. before the other siblings arrive, one picks out the best pieces from the mother's jewellery. This behaviour may be a result of "inner accounting": an attempt to compensate after their death for the love or attention not received during the parents' life—even at the cost of close relatives feeling betrayed. Grievance and hurt can escalate to feelings of hatred and rupture. The term "emotional messiness" accurately describes this conglomeration of emotional storms that are difficult to differentiate and to which the actors are sometimes exposed. These are not just temporary states of emotional tension but a persistent mix of intense negative feelings experienced by the family members.[17]

2.4 The "Duplicated" Family

A business family faces the same issues as every other family: organising events in the family life cycle, raising children, and balancing the relationships between different generations: in other words, being a "normal family". At the same time, the constant presence of the company forces them to be part of another social system, that of the business family.[18] They manage the paradoxical expectation to care for their members as any other family does while also observing their members continuously in terms of what their development, friends, and behaviour might mean for the company. The business family must constantly oscillate between family issues and business issues; it must be at the same time a private,

---

[17] Brundin and Sharma (2012).
[18] Remember that in the case of the Abel family, we explained that there might be two communication systems in the room: four people but two system logics.

Fig. 2.3 The two sides of the business family

emotionally connected family and a business family, both forms of family and yet completely different. The family must, so to speak, "duplicate itself"[19] and become "two families", viewing its members as "normal family" members on the one hand while always observing and evaluating their behaviour as a "business family" on the other. This situation is illustrated in Fig. 2.3.

> In a particularly striking example, the successor to a small German technology business had received a Fischer construction kit as a Christmas present when he was six years old. He enthusiastically set to work and began to tinker with it. "Suddenly," he reports, "I felt that something was weird. I looked up and saw six adults looking at me as if spellbound, watching my play. At the time I didn't understand what it was, but now I know—at that moment, they weren't looking at me as a happy child, they were looking at me thinking that, with my enthusiasm for technical matters, I might be suitable for the succession." He experienced first-hand what it means being as a member of a "duplicated family" exposed to "double observation": his relatives enjoyed his pleasure in the gift (family perspective) but at the same time saw his potential suitability as successor (business family perspective). Actually, he finally took over the company after his studies.

---

[19] von Schlippe et al. (2021).

It is important to mention one more aspect here: the "duplication" of the family is a way of intuitively handling paradoxical complexity. The family is generally not aware of the oscillation: they are simply thinking over breakfast about whether or not to purchase the new machine and the operative member may therefore react irritably when the topic of the flunked class assignment is brought up: "Don't give me something like that now!"

2.5 So, Why Not Say: "Family and Business Don't Work Together!"

From a theoretical perspective, the complex combination of the "family business" should not work at all. If we consider the contradictory nature of the logics involved, conflict in business families should be the norm. What really needs to be explained, therefore, is how so many business families manage—contrary to the theory—to get along well with each other to some extent, and this does seem to be the case. Obviously, members of business families are often able to endure the paradoxes described or even transform them into a special resource.

At the same time, it is anything but a fault if a family finds it difficult to cope with the complexity briefly outlined here, and becomes caught up in conflict. "It happens in the best of families," as the saying goes.[20] And once a conflict has taken root in the family, it is difficult to banish it. The family can then become an emotional arena in which the conflict dynamics that unfold put great strain on those involved, especially because, typically, without being aware of it, family members become caught up in a maelstrom of events over which they have less and less control. Those involved think that they are still in charge and acting with clarity, but something else has long since taken command—the conflict dynamics.

It should have become clear to the reader that it is almost impossible for members of business families *not* to come into conflict or conflictual

---

[20] This phrase was used as the title for von Schlippe (2014).

communication over time, particularly in the context of succession planning, if not before. The decisive factor in whether a massive escalation, rift, and subsequent sale of parts of or the whole business will occur is the overall attitude to conflict within the family. A family may see dissent, disagreement, divergent attitudes, and opinions as an integral part of (business-) family life that ensures future viability. Family management may then aim at resolving conflicts professionally and constructively. If, on the other hand, a family sees conflict as something that mustn't ever happen, the members aren't well prepared if they occur. So, in essence, business families might better learn to accept conflicts as an inescapable concomitant of the connection between family and company, to learn how to handle them in a constructive way,[21] and not be too afraid for them to come.

2.6 Conclusion: The Business Family as an "Emotional Arena"

It has long been recognised that organisations in general and family businesses in particular are anything but havens of rationality and objectivity and that they can, rather, be seen as "emotional arenas" in which people are thrown together with varying feelings and subjective experience, bringing their emotions with them.[22] Almost all organisational processes—even those that are purely objective from a formal perspective—are interlaced with emotions. This fact does not generally correspond well to the logic of a business in which actions are at least supposed to be "rational". Even though it may now be clear that we are talking about "bounded rationality", the aim will nonetheless usually be to banish feelings from the business sphere as a source of irrationality.

Feelings are, of course, just as virulent in business families. The paradoxical tension between the differing logics of the systems of family,

---

[21] We often recommend that families familiarise themselves with the concept of nonviolent communication (e.g. Rosenberg & Chopra, 2015).
[22] Brundin and Härtel (2014), Zellweger (2017).

business, and owners has already been mentioned above. It quickly becomes clear that feelings have very different roles to play within these logics and are treated very differently. In the context of a business, powerful feelings can be interpreted as indicating unresolved organisational issues. In family businesses, this might suggest that a successful balance has not—or not yet—been struck between the paradoxes arising from the interlinking of the systems as described above. Of course—and it is worth emphasising this once again here—the context of the family business also offers a wealth of opportunity for positive feelings and experiences. Owning a business and being associated with its name and shared history can be a happy, fulfilling experience. Many families explicitly want their businesses to contribute meaningfully to society and take on social responsibility. The family business then provides the family with a constructive challenge to which it can collectively rise. The business is felt to be an important part of the family's identity. Family members may have a sense of pride in being a part of this and experience "psychological ownership" or—more specifically in the case of family businesses—"emotional ownership".[23] The family will be happy to bask in the reputation associated with the name of the business.

If we are to examine the theme of conflict in family businesses, however, we must also turn our attention to negative emotions. As discussed, those involved in these complex systems constantly find themselves in "paradoxical" situations: what is right in the logic of one system is wrong in that of the other. A good solution according to one logic (e.g. excluding a person who lacks aptitude from the management) may be experienced as hurtful and as a personal rejection in the other logic. The protagonists are often not aware that they are operating in contexts which are, in a way, "impossible". The many family business paradoxes are experienced emotionally and are of course also reflected in communication. Individuals may feel personally hurt with regard to very fundamental issues: their life's work and long-standing loyalty are at stake, as well as the recognition or disparagement of these things, with associated feelings of love, disappointment, and betrayal. These emotions tend to be focused

---

[23] Björnberg and Nicholson (2012).

on specific individuals: this or the other person "caused" somebody to feel a certain way; they are "to blame"—"your fault!". The assumption of this book, however, is that emotions—including negative ones—can be regarded, systemically speaking, as the "immune system" within the overall system. In this case, strong feelings can certainly be interpreted as an important warning signal that an imbalance remains between the family and business logics. It makes little progress for individual members in the family to blame each other.

All these aspects form a basis for the emergence of conflict. Once a conflict has started, its development follows certain psychological laws that are well known and have been thoroughly studied in conflict research. Nevertheless, the actors are often unaware that their conflict behaviour is not at all rational but frequently follows dynamics that are prescribed by the conflict. The following section will sketch out the mostly foreseeable—and, for conflict experts, almost predictable—courses of conflicts.

References

Bateson, G., Jackson, D., Haley, J., & Weakland, J. (1956). Toward a theory of schizophrenia. *Behavioral Science, 1*, 151–261.
Björnberg, A., & Nicholson, N. (2012). Emotional ownership: The next generation's relationship with the family firm. *Family Business Review, 25*(4), 374–390.
Boszormenyi-Nagy, I., & Spark, G. (1973). *Invisible loyalties. Reciprocity in intergenerational family therapy.* Harper & Row.
Brundin, E., & Härtel, C. (2014). Emotions in family firms. In L. Melin, M. Nordqvist, & P. Sharma (Eds.), *The SAGE handbook of family business* (pp. 529–548). Sage.
Brundin, E., & Sharma, P. (2012). Love, hate, and desire: The role of emotional messiness in the business family. In A. L. Carsrud & M. Brännback (Eds.), *Understanding family businesses* (pp. 55–71). Springer.
Chua, J. H., Chrisman, J. J., & Sharma, P. (1999). Defining the family business by behavior. *Entrepreneurship Theory and Practice, 23*(1), 19–39.
Kleve, H., Roth, S., Köllner, T., & Wetzel, R. (2020). The tetralemma of the business family: A systemic approach to business-family dilemmas in research and practice. *Journal of Organizational Change Management, 33*(2), 433–446.

Leaptrott, J. (2005). An institutional theory view of the family business. *Family Business Review, 18*(3), 215–228.
Litz, R. (2012). Double roles, double binds? Double bind theory and family business research. In A. Carsrud & M. Brännback (Eds.), *Understanding family business. Unique perspectives, neglected topics, and undiscovered approaches* (pp. 115–132). Springer.
Luhmann, N. (1995). *Social systems*. Stanford University Press.
Luhmann, N. (2000). *Organisation und Entscheidung*. Westdeutscher Verlag.
Montada, L. (2003). Justice, equity and fairness. In J. Weiner (Ed.), *Handbook of psychology* (Vol. 5, pp. 537–568). Wiley.
Rosenberg, M., & Chopra, D. (2015). *Nonviolent communication: A language of life* (3rd ed.). PuddleDancer Press.
Schuman, A., Stutz, S., & Ward, J. L. (2010). *Family business as paradox* (pp. 22–29). Palgrave Macmillan.
Tagiuri, R., & Davis, J. (1996). Bivalent attributes of the family firm. *Family Business Review, 9*(2), 199–208.
von Schlippe, A. (2014). *Das kommt in den besten Familien vor. Systemische Konfliktberatung in Familien und Familienunternehmen* (1. Aufl.). Concadora.
von Schlippe, A. (2022). Das Testament schafft Fakten. Erben, Vererbung und Gerechtigkeit. *Familiendynamik, 47*(1), 4–11.
von Schlippe, A., & Frank, H. (2013). The theory of social systems as a framework for understanding family businesses. *Family Relations, 62*(3), 384–398.
von Schlippe, A., & Frank, H. (2017). Conflict in family business in the light of systems theory. In F. Kellermanns & F. Hoy (Eds.), *The Routledge companion to family business* (pp. 367–384). Routledge.
von Schlippe, A., Rüsen, T., & Groth, T. (2021). *The two sides of the business family. Governance and strategy across generations*. Springer.
Watzlawick, P., Beavin, J. B., & Jackson, D. D. (1969). *Pragmatics of human communication: A study of interactional patterns, pathologies and paradoxes*. WW Norton & Company.
Wimmer, R. (2014). Wie familiär sind Familienunternehmen? In O. Geramanis & K. Hermann (Eds.), *Organisation und Intimität* (pp. 25–40). Carl Auer Systeme.
Zellweger, T. (2017). *Managing the family business. Theory and practice*. Edward Elgar.

3

Typical Conflict: Courses and Mechanisms

Conflicts are as diverse in content as the people involved and their different interests. This diversity cannot be reproduced here, and this guide does not in any case aim to address questions of specific content; there are many guides available on ideal succession plans and appropriate distribution levels. The aim here is, rather, to show the basic structures of conflict processes to help families break out of vicious circles of escalation. Those who realise that they are caught in one of these typical dynamics, which follow well-known patterns almost independently of the individual, are no longer quite so subject to (or even "victim" of) the course of the conflict. Quite apart from this, a prior awareness can prevent the corresponding course of events from ever arising: "forewarned is forearmed". We believe that the best way to prevent crises in a business family (besides contractual regulations) is to establish a shared knowledge of the nature, course, and typical escalation scenarios in business families.

3.1 Attributing the Cause to a Single Person and the Insinuation of Motives

> Key Phrase:
> Attributing complexity to a single person increases escalation.

The terms in the heading may be unfamiliar but are not hard to understand. As described above, business families are faced with a particular complexity that is challenging to manage. Here, the human mind tends to resort to the tried and tested, but highly questionable, method of simplification: in the face of complexity that is difficult to understand, people tend to "miscalculate". What could be more obvious than blaming the other person for the mess and attributing the cause of the conflict to them—"It's all your fault!" Psychologically, it is, in any case, easier not to perceive one's own role in the dynamics of the conflict. That is why personal related attribution is so popular. At the same time, it escalates the situation because the other person usually reacts in a similar way. The situation is further exacerbated when motives are assumed; people are sometimes convinced they can "see into" the other person's head and "know" their motives better than they do themselves ("Yes, I hear you say that, but I know better: you're only doing this because …"). It becomes particularly dramatic when these alleged motivations are underpinned by "hobby psychology": "You're acting like a child, what's wrong with you?"; "I know you never could cope with the fact that …"; "You need to work through your mother complex somewhere else"; "You are the perfect example of a narcissist".

And, let's be honest, it really is true! (isn't it?):

- "It's his fault—he's responsible."
- "If (s)he only changed their mind, that would solve everything."
- "The fact that he won't back down proves he must be stupid, insane or evil, diabolic."

As already stated, tragically, both sides tend to settle conflicts in this way (and try to persuade the moderator to decide who is wrong). This is the first ticket to escalation. The more one party is convinced that it is the other's fault—while the other "foolishly" thinks the reverse—the faster the escalation spirals get out of control. The missing link is self-reflexivity.

Figure 3.1 shows as a caricature a situation that in reality did happen step by step (and not on a couch): two brothers each told the counsellor in a separate interview their opinion about the opponent. The pattern described here was very clear: the "bad" one and the "mad" one…

Exercise 1
Imagine a conflict and think about the words you would use to describe the other person/the other party. How many of these words fit in the category of "stupid, insane, or evil"? What changes if you think about the following sentence: "There are no evil people, only entangled ones"? (At least we may have to admit that the entanglement can have become very knotted!).

My brother is a criminal   My brother urgently needs a psychiatrist

Fig. 3.1 Two brothers at the psychiatrist

Exercise 2
Think of a conflict and consider to whom you attribute which proportion of the "blame" for it. You probably attribute none to yourself, or perhaps just a small amount of "partial blame". What changes if you attribute 50% of the blame for the situation to yourself and 50% to the other person involved? How does this change your thinking, your perspective on the conflict and the next steps?

3.2 Errors in Social Perception

> **Key Phrase:**
> In conflict, cognitive function begins to narrow and the other person will be increasingly described in demonic terms.

Two mechanisms of social psychology particularly aggravate the development of a conflict: *fundamental* and *hostile* "perception-" or "attribution-errors". These refer to people's tendency to perceive and interpret what goes on around them in a certain way. "Attributions" are assumptions about causal correlations in the world around us. Their mental purpose is to create order: things, elements, and people are linked to each other in such a way that they appear meaningful to the individual in question.

When people lack certainty, they apply causal attributions with a particular intensity. This is logical: when we are confused and uncertain, we seek guidance as quickly as possible. Disputes based on paradoxes, as we have seen, are often highly affectively charged, while at the same time being impenetrable and disconcerting. Both fundamental and hostile perception errors (also called "attribution errors") are concerned with an individual's tendency to see the opponent in a certain way, one that fosters escalation.

The Fundamental Perceptual Error
The first of these errors in perception leads directly to conflict.[1] It is linked to the very human characteristic of attributing good events as far as possible to oneself ("We won this game due to my outstanding skills as a striker") while seeking the causes of negative events elsewhere ("We lost because the pitch was awful/the ref was unfair/the goalie messed up"). In cases of conflict, people tend to judge other people's behaviour as an expression of their character: "That just shows again how thoroughly nasty he is!", while their own behaviour is seen simply as a reaction to that of the other side: "I didn't like it but I had to act in that way!" The same action is thus perceived as totally different: for the opponent, "What a bad move by him!" but for me, "I had no choice but to hit him." We always choose descriptions that show ourselves to have moral integrity.

In this logic, the other person has to take the blame for their own negative behaviour and its consequences and is increasingly demonised, that is, described in an exclusively negative way.[2] As a result, when the level of escalation is high, we can act badly towards the other person with a clean conscience—after all, it's them! They are the "bad guy"; they "didn't want it any other way"; that is "probably the only language they understand"! In this context, the Austrian conflict researcher Fritz Glasl speaks of "demonised zones", in which both sides act without taking responsibility: "I had to break his bones, he didn't want it any other way!" Whenever you hear yourself making such arguments, consider it a red alert!

The escalation carousel is dramatically accelerated.[3] Since the perceptions of the other are equally distorted, they see every action as a sign of the conflict partner's evil and think that they "only have to react". If the degree of escalation is very high, both sides may engage in destructive

---

[1] Berry and Frederickson (2015).
[2] Alon and Omer (2006).
[3] The "carousel of outrage and indignation" is the core metaphor for escalating conflict in von Schlippe (2022).

"acting without taking responsibility"; both see themselves as "forced" to do so by the other.

The Hostile Perceptual Error

While the fundamental error leads directly to conflict and escalation, the hostile attributional error prevents any escape: "Hostile attitudes and perceptions tend to endure once established because they support each other".[4] This error is characterised by the fact that we essentially see the other person as negative and are no longer willing to impute any positive motives to them.[5] Neutral behaviour—or even a positive step by the other person, such as an offer—is interpreted as a trap. In the grip of the hostile perceptual error, perception narrows and negative expectation structures develop, affecting communication. For example, an attempt at de-escalation or a proposal for reconciliation by the conflict partner may be scornfully rejected: "Oh, now you're going to try it that way? Not with me, I'm not falling for that!" The door slams shut, and the chance for clarification is lost; worse still, the conciliatory party is now even more deeply offended and turns the escalation screw for his part: "That's the last time I'll try to make it up with you. Now nothing will hold me back, I'll show you!" For the other person, this proves once again that they were right in their original assessment. The literature talks of "self-fulfilling prophecies" here: "Now you're showing your true colours. I knew you didn't mean it seriously—you were just faking!" The negative mutual impressions of one another are once again confirmed and the conflict has deepened, although the offer of reconciliation might have been meant seriously as a genuine way out.

> Example: In the above-mentioned counselling of the two hostile brothers, one says to the adviser in a one-on-one conversation, "... and imagine the cheek, he invites me to his 60th birthday!" When asked in astonishment whether this was, in fact, simply a friendly gesture, he responds, "Ah, you don't know him; he just wants to make me look ridiculous in front of his guests." After we had discussed the error, a question made him think: "Supposing your brother really is sincere, would you give him a chance?"— and he became willing to at least imagine that there could be several ways of interpreting the invitation differently.

Fig. 3.2 The hostile attributional error and demonised zones

The perceptual errors described above are essentially psychological mechanisms that create blind spots: they make our own part in the conflict invisible, even to ourselves. They are tragic in that they drive an ever-increasing escalation.

Acknowledging the existence of these two perceptual errors—alongside developing an internal family "sensorium" through which their corresponding dynamics can be detected in burgeoning conflicts—helps the business family to make these errors visible and, ideally, manageable. Alertness to these basic psychological patterns, which are independent of the individual, is a valuable form of conflict prevention in business families and may help prevent families from falling blindly into the traps of perceptual errors which leave them at the mercy of an escalation of the conflict they cause (Fig. 3.2).

3.3 Violated Sense of Justice and Indignation

Key Phrase:
When the sense of justice is violated, clear thinking stops.

In Human Relations

Social conflicts arise from the violation of expectations that are considered "fair" by those involved, as discussed in the first part of this text. As a rule, conflict is caused by a violated sense of justice on both sides.[6] It is important to realise that "justice" does not exist independently: it is a social construction, an abstraction that can never be achieved universally. Rather, it must be related to a concrete situation and, ultimately, negotiated accordingly. There are probably as many different ideas of what is fair and just as there are people in the world (see also Sect. 2.3 about the "Paradox of justice").

The violation of justice is felt painfully—a consciousness of justice is probably deeply ingrained in us. The "belief in a just world", the claim that the world should—indeed *must*—be fair, strongly motivates most people[7] and gives rise to indignation and outrage. Indignation is not a feeling, but a physical reaction to one's own thoughts, a so-called "self-hypnosis"—"Unbelievable, what is he thinking, but now it's over!". Sometimes this phenomenon is called a "secondary feeling"—we experience it as a feeling without being aware of how our mental mistakes have contributed.[8] This is a dangerous psychological mechanism: those who are angry, indignant, and outraged believe themselves to be absolutely in the right; they tend to demonise the other party (see previous section), seeing themselves as entitled to act destructively without taking responsibility for their actions.

Tragically, this perspective, and feelings about justice or just solutions to a situation, are usually not expressed. Not only in business families do we have no "communicative arenas" in which such a debate would be possible in a structured way. Often, each family member remains alone with their individual notion of what is fair and sees no way to express their feelings of injustice in a conflict-neutral way. These feelings thus ferment until the last straw breaks the camel's back and, suddenly, feelings that have festered for years or even decades are articulated—and come out then with an explosion. The best prevention would be the creation of specific communicative spaces at regular intervals, with professional moderation—by a trained family member or external confidant.

---

[6] Montada (2003).
[7] Succinctly illustrated by Lerner (1980).
[8] Greenberg (2015).

This may help to manage emerging feelings, impressions, or the processing of problematic decisions within the family. Families are often afraid of intense emotions and put off conversations about them—but then, at critical points (such as inheritance), when the topic is on the table, emotions flare up, giving reason to be even more cautious and afraid the next time. We recommend that business families organise a regular "family laundry day" (e.g. a moderated workshop) once a year. This may help to process the latent conflict potential in moderate doses (e.g. by talking about justice in a situation before the will is known) and to develop a constructive attitude towards conflict in general.

3.4 Psychological Contracts

As mentioned earlier, the topic of justice is key to understanding difficult conflict situations; indeed, *every* conflict is probably based on a mutual experience of injustice. Sometimes the violation of a *psychological contract* may be the cause of conflict, usually between generations. In general, this concept describes implicit agreements that are never made clear, which are later recalled in very different ways. Psychological contracts are implicit, vague (sometimes even intentionally) promises or hints ("Let's get started, we will agree on the rest later") made for a distant future. The term comes from organisational psychology[9] and describes implicit expectations regarding, for example, future salary or career options. An employee may develop certain expectations on the basis of such hints. Mostly, however, these "contracts" are perceived—and, above all, remembered—very differently by each side. In a study, 55% of employees, in various companies, report having experienced a "psychological contract violation" or a "broken promise", a dramatic figure.[10]

When working with business families, we often see recognition and consternation when the topic of psychological contracts is raised. It is precisely within families that such promises occur and are often made in a typical family fashion: "One day, dear child, you will …". The parent may not even remember the scene; for the child, it may impact their

---

[9] Hülsbeck and von Schlippe (2018).
[10] Robinson and Rousseau (1994).

entire life plan and career. It can become very difficult when the life plans of members of a business family, made based on such vague promises, come to a dead end: a course of studies that wasn't their first choice, career opportunities declined while waiting for "the day to come"—and then, instead, huge disappointment (the so-called successor's trap).[11]

The problem is that these agreements are taken for granted at least from one side. For one party, it was maybe just a throwaway statement, made on a whim: "Who knows, someday you'll be the boss here"; for the other, it had the character of a promise: "Yes! Someday I'll be the boss here." Since both assume their memory of the conversation is the only possible one, they usually discuss no further what may have meant in this implicit promise. Both take their own versions for granted and, therefore, no longer question them.

The non-fulfilment of such an agreement—which one side may not even see as such—can lead to an intensely felt sense of violated justice, rising to a high level of indignation, with the consequences discussed in the previous section.

If it concerns only a promised piece of jewellery ("Someday your wife will wear this ring"), a broken psychological contract may perhaps still be tolerated. It is different with larger assets or when a career is planned and a life path chosen based on an implicit promise that ends in nothing.

> In the example of the two hostile brothers ("He's invited me to his birthday"), the psychological contract could be reconstructed as follows. One, having become the managing director, remembered the implicit promise of his father, who died when he was 24: "You will take over the business!" The other (a non-executive partner) perceived the contract differently: "There will always be absolute equality between you." These two personal readings led to conflict: every major action taken by one, as CEO, was questioned by his brother, who felt he should have equal input into key decisions regarding the business. This, in turn, infuriated the other: his brother was not an active shareholder and should be happy with his shares and let him get on with the job! Each felt a sense of deep injustice in the other's actions, reading in them a lack of recognition of their own role.

---

[11] Kaye (1996).

One day I will entrust all this to you!

Fig. 3.3 Psychological contracts: One day, my son…

As in the challenges of addressing expectations of justice and perceptions of injustice presented in the last section, it may be useful for business families to identify confidants, structures, and arenas that allow expectations to be addressed and potential breaks in existing psychological contracts to be highlighted (Fig. 3.3).

3.5 Momentum of Escalation: The "Parasite"

> **Key Phrase:**
> At some point, "We have a conflict" becomes "The conflict has us".

One aspect of conflict is often underestimated—its inherent dynamism. The mechanisms outlined so far usually apply to both parties in the conflict and have a direct effect on communication. The parties involved are caught in a vicious circle in which their psychological conditions change without them even being aware of it. The negative effect of stress on cognitive function has been known for over half a century now: the body activates hormones and neurotransmitters that shut down the prefrontal cortex. This limits access to more complex knowledge content, our thinking, and, especially, access to memory content: "Under stress, rigid 'habit' memory is favoured over more flexible 'cognitive' memory"[12] and all this because "memories are highly dynamic entities. After initial encoding, memories remain fragile, and susceptible to numerous amnesic agents or modifications by new information."[13]

The field of vision narrows; communication gets interrupted or at least impoverished—thereby providing "a greenhouse in which rumors flourish".[14] The ability to imagine how things look from the other person's perspective gets lost; one becomes unable to empathise with the other position. So-called "affective-cognitive private worlds" develop, that is, very individual views of reality that are experienced as absolute truths.[15] These private worlds can develop in an individual but can also be found in groups (e.g. in a family or a team) and are then also referred to as "group-think". Self-control is also impaired; reactions become impulsive and uncontrolled, even to the point of fearing oneself: "I would never have thought I was capable of doing this!" Increasingly, the communication system is poisoned; more and more areas of hitherto undisturbed everyday communication are affected ("Could you pass the salt, please?"—"Get it yourself!") and statements that were meant positively are twisted. It is a spiral that is hard to escape, at least without help.[16]

System theory has an interesting term for this dynamic: the conflict is seen as a "parasite".[17] It worms its way into the communication system, so to speak, feeds on it, and, at the same time, destroys it from within. Usual forms of interaction dissolve: those involved no longer hold the

---

[12] Schwabe et al. (2010, p. 584).
[13] Quaedflieg and Schwabe (2018, p. 364).
[14] Pruitt and Kim (2004, p. 160).
[15] Ciompi and Endert (2011).
[16] Glasl (1999).
[17] Luhmann (1995).

door open for each other when entering a room at the same time, and no longer hand each other the salt when asked for it. The metaphor is interesting and illustrates the momentum: "the parasite seizes power". The individual believes they are acting rationally and thoughtfully, but their communication patterns and culture of interacting are already "eaten away and destroyed by the parasite".

The consequence for conflict counselling is significant: after a certain point, what matters is no longer the issue at hand, but simply winning—or, at least, not losing. The conflict is maintained by the hope of winning or, if that is no longer possible, then at least damaging or even destroying the other person. These are fantasies into which the parasite seduces those involved. Conflict resolution at this stage is, therefore, about bringing the quarrelling partners together to fight the parasite together: It is not the opponent who is the real enemy; *the real enemy is the parasite*—the escalating conflict dynamic that prevents both from finding a joint solution. The more they surrender to the parasite and its demands, the greater the destruction will be; the challenge is whether they can unite to fight the parasite together (Fig. 3.4).

Fig. 3.4 The conflict as a "parasite" in the business family

What can a business family do to protect itself from a "parasite infestation"? First of all, it is important to recognise the parasite for what it is: a pattern originally created by the people involved that has gradually taken more and more control, so that it has now grown beyond their control. If we succeed in applying the metaphor of the parasite, it can be made visible and approachable for all family members and, importantly, it is seen as a joint "project", a psychological mechanism, and no one's fault. When we ask whether business families have been afflicted by this parasite, few deny it. Sometimes it may even be helpful to give this specific dynamic, this "ugly pet" that has taken place within their relationship a name so that it can be addressed with a wink. If this is successful, the family can then analyse what the parasite in their particular family feeds on. A good counselling question[18] for this would be, "Imagine you wake up and the conflict has disappeared. It has dissolved overnight; it is simply gone. What would you have to do, how would you have to act to make 'ugly pet' come back, to keep it going?"

This may sound too simple, and it is (as is the cartoon 3.4). It is not easy to eradicate the hurt caused by offences, ironic and rude remarks, or even malicious actions. The essential step, though, is the joint decision to restore a culture of respect within the family and not allow the conflict, the parasite to take control: "No matter how difficult the conflict, we all have the chance to work on improving the culture of being in contact and talking to each other!"

3.6 Escalation Stages and the "Four Horsemen of the Apocalypse"

Key Phrase:
It's not difficult to fall into the abyss: just go down, a bit faster, step by step—there'll be no way back!

---

[18] This so-called "reverse miracle question" is suggested by F. B. Simon.

3 Typical Conflict: Courses and Mechanisms   49

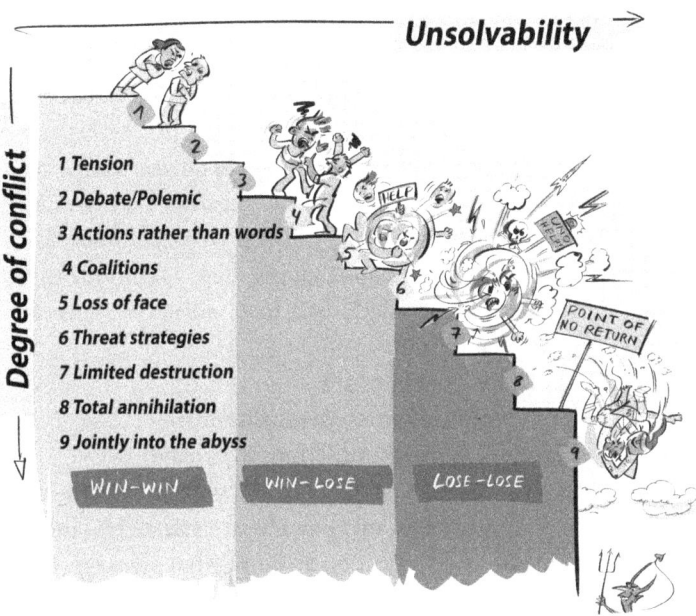

Fig. 3.5 The ladder into the abyss

To assess the pull of the depths that grip people in conflict situations, the conflict researcher Friedrich Glasl presented a memorable "ladder to the abyss".[19] It comprises nine steps (see Fig. 3.5).

In the first two or three steps, the system can generally find its way back to a cooperative basis on its own and a win-win outcome (i.e. one from which both parties benefit) is often possible. The first three stages are:

1. Hardening.
2. Debate.
3. Actions: Action instead of words!

---

[19] Glasl (1999).

Step 3 is an important turning point. From the fourth stage onwards, it tends to be difficult to find a way back alone; outside help is needed. A particularly critical threshold is reached between Stages 4 and 5, where facts are increasingly abandoned, and the factual conflict turns into a relationship conflict. This stage is characterised by increasingly personal attacks ("Are you just pretending or are you really that stupid?"; "You're obviously insane!"). It is no longer about the original conflict issues any more, but about saving face. Without outside help, there is the threat of a so-called "win-lose" situation: one side loses. The steps continue as follows:

4. Images and coalitions (rumour mill).
5. Loss of face (termination of trust, demonisation).
6. Threatening strategies (threats and counter-threats).

From about the seventh stage, the parasite has definitely taken absolute control. The mutual injuries are so extensive—and the need for compensation or restoration so strong—that damage to, or even the destruction of, the other is accepted, even at the price of one's own destruction. Here, as a rule, separation and interruption by external agents are necessary ("the deployment of the UN"); without help, these phases usually end in "lose-lose" outcomes with the destruction of social and other forms of capital.

7. Limited destruction strikes to damage the other/the other side.
8. Massive annihilation strikes to destroy the other/the other side.
9. Together into the abyss; the goal is now to destroy the other/the other side, even at the cost of self-destruction (psychological, financial, yes, even physical).

The last stage is tragic, not only in business families but especially here: it results in a "family war".[20] The media is full of examples where family members have unthinkingly risked the fate of the business and, thus, also that of those working there and their families. In order to harm the other party, the destruction of the business is accepted.

---

[20] Gordon and Nicholson (2008).

> In the example of the two quarrelling brothers mentioned above, the degree to which Level 9 was achieved is seen in the following account. When the conflict counsellors became aware of the danger the business was in (approvals had not been given for necessary investments, annual financial statements and plans were no longer formally approved, etc.), they advised, "If you continue like this, the business will go under." The non-managing shareholder and brother of the CEO responded, "So what? When we both will have nothing left, then justice will finally be done."

The degree of escalation can also be assessed on the basis of the so-called "horsemen of the apocalypse", who are said to announce the impending end of the world. The American couple therapist John Gottman has identified several communication features that indicate these "horsemen".[21] He claimed that he could predict with 95% certainty whether a couple would divorce within the following 2 years from watching a video of a five-minute argument, in which he would observe the interactions, noting these characteristics:

- Unrestrained criticism, blame, and accusations. The opponent is criticised without consideration, he or she will be described as defective, meaning the "face" (the self-esteem of the other) is continuously attacked.
- Defence, justification, denial of own share of blame, and counter-criticism; critical remarks of the other person are immediately rejected without thinking about potential truth, often paired with justifications or counter blames. Own responsibility is constantly denied.
- Contempt: no more respect for each other, and sarcasm and cynicism come to the fore. This horseman is considered the most dangerous; paradoxically, it appears with a decrease in conflict intensity, when the couple no longer care about each other and simply do not talk to each other. Contempt is a strong predictor of poor well-being, illness, and divorce.
- Blocking: this manifests itself physically in turning away, silence, freezing out, and closing up, so that the other person is talking to a brick wall: it isn't even worth time or effort to fight for a better relationship.

---

[21] Gottman (1994).

The more of these "riders" are on the move, the less optimism is indicated.

Due to the high risk that conflicts of Level 4 or higher pose to the cohesion and survival of the family business, we consider a knowledge of Glasl's conflict model and Gottman's "horsemen" to be central components of any training and further education concepts for professional ownership. These enable business family members to identify the degree of escalation in an existing conflict and to decide which forms of conflict management are still viable.

3.7 The Transgenerational Transmission of Conflict Histories

> Key Phrase:
> Inherited conflicts are the hardest to resolve.

Some conflicts, unfortunately, do not resolve themselves over time but are passed on to future generations, and these are usually particularly difficult to deal with. Like the blood feuds of the past, the actual cause might long be forgotten; only the hereditary enmity remains: "they" have always rejected "us", taken advantage of us, etc. In multi-generational business families, unresolved tension can be passed on in subfamilies in the form of stories ("the communicative memory of the social system", as Luhmann quoted it), keeping the feud alive. The children who hear these stories do not usually understand that there could be another, equally convincing, version of the story. They generally identify wholeheartedly with the narrator, to whom they are attached or whom they love, sharing their narrator's indignation and, thus, perpetuating the conflict.

> Stefanie L, an influential individual shareholder, showed exactly this indignation: "Why should I agree to this transaction? You have already rejected my father and grandfather. But now that you need my vote, I am meant to forget all that? I am not prepared to do that."

Knowing about conflict stories, their versions and the solutions that have been found to help overcome the conflicts they cause is, therefore, another key form of building conflict resilience for the business family. It can help to delve into the family history and understand how the business family as a whole has managed not to fall prey to typical causes of conflict or has mastered conflict situations that have arisen.

3.8 Threatened Sense of Belonging

The need to belong is fundamental to human existence.[22] It is one of the most important of human needs, although it is often explicitly excluded from business logic (even though there are organisations that specifically exploit this need, e.g. those structured like sects). Businesses are very selective and the question "Who is in, who is out?" is frequently asked. Hiring, firing, general staffing decisions, and board appointments are day-to-day business occurrences. Even though human resource managers know all too well the effect that a dismissal can have on a person, organisational logic ultimately takes precedence.

In a family, however, the need to belong is existential: calling it into question causes childhood feelings and fundamental fears to take over and, from the emotional perspective, a person's very survival is at stake. Even though it is not possible to be excluded from a family itself, in the context of a family business the refusal of a position in management, on the advisory board, or in asset succession may be subjectively experienced as a dramatic exclusion, possibly with lasting consequences. It remains an ongoing challenge for family strategy to strike a balance between natural affiliation (family logic) on the one hand and selectivity around appointments (business logic) on the other. Naming the dilemma openly and acknowledging that any solution will imply negative feelings may be the first step towards a family discussion about these issues.

---

[22] Baumeister and Leary (1995).

> Example: "You're out!": An entrepreneur appointed his daughter and, albeit with hesitation, his son as his successors to run the company together because he believed he had to do equal justice to both.. It was not a success: the siblings did not get along with each other and divisions formed among staff. Numerous attempts to resolve the problem (creating separate sections, establishing a defined area of work for the brother) were unsuccessful. Finally, the sister and her father—who still held shares in the company—decided to dismiss the brother, as they did not believe he had the qualities required of a manager. A shareholder meeting was held at which the dismissal was the only agenda item and the motion to dismiss the brother was passed (as father and daughter together held 67% of the shares it was a clear vote but nevertheless very offending for the brother). He took such offence at this and was so permanently aggrieved that, from then on, he used his share of the vote to repeatedly sabotage his sister's plans, and still held sufficient sway to be able to block any larger-scale decision.

References

Alon, N., & Omer, H. (2006). *The psychology of demonization: Promoting acceptance and reducing conflict*. Routledge.

Baumeister, R. F., & Leary, M. R. (1995). The need to belong: Desire for interpersonal attachments as a fundamental human motivation. *Psychological Bulletin, 117*(3), 497–529.

Berry, Z., & Frederickson, J. (2015). Explanations and implications of the fundamental attribution error: A review and proposal. *Journal of Integrated Social Sciences, 5*(1), 44–57.

Ciompi, L., & Endert, E. (2011). *Gefühle machen Geschichte. Die Wirkung kollektiver Emotionen – von Hitler bis Obama*. Vandenhoeck & Ruprecht.

Dodge, K. (2006). Translational science in action: Hostile attributional style and the development of aggressive behavior problems. *Development and Psychopathology, 18*, 791–814.

Glasl, F. (1999). *Confronting conflict. A first aid kit for handling conflict*. Hawthorne.

Gordon, G., & Nicholson, N. (2008). *Family wars: Classic conflicts in family business and how to deal with them*. Kogan.

Gottman, J. M. (1994). *What predicts divorce? The relationship between marital processes and marital outcomes*. Lawrence Erlbaum.

Greenberg, L. (2015). *Emotion-focused therapy: Coaching clients to work through their feelings* (2nd ed.). American Psychological Association.

Hülsbeck, M., & von Schlippe, A. (2018). Die Rolle psychologischer Kontrakte für die Entstehung von Konflikten. *Konfliktdynamik, 7*(2), 92–101.

Kaye, K. (1996). When the family business is a sickness. *Family Business Review, 9*(4), 347–368.

Lerner, M. J. (1980). *The belief in a just world: A fundamental delusion.* Plenum Press.

Luhmann, N. (1995). *Social systems.* Stanford University Press.

Montada, L. (2003). Justice, equity and fairness. In J. Weiner (Ed.), *Handbook of psychology* (Vol. 5, pp. 537–568). Wiley.

Pruitt, D., & Kim, S. H. (2004). *Social conflict: Escalation, stalemate, and settlement* (3rd ed.). McGrawhill.

Quaedflieg, C., & Schwabe, L. (2018). Memory dynamics under stress. *Memory, 26*(3), 364–376.

Robinson, S. L., & Rousseau, D. M. (1994). Violating the psychological contract: Not the exception but the norm. *Journal of Organizational Behavior, 15*, 249–259.

Schwabe, L., Wolf, O., & Oitzl, M. (2010). Memory formation under stress: Quantity and quality. *Neuroscience & Biobehavioral Reviews, 34*(4), 584–591.

von Schlippe, A. (2022). *Das Karussell der Empörung. Eskalierte Konflikte verstehen und begrenzen.* Vandenhoeck & Ruprecht.

4

Dealing with Conflicts on the Individual Level: Unfollow the Prescribed Patterns

At this point, we cannot offer any detailed instructions on how to deal with conflicts, but only help in trying to repair a damaged dynamic within family communication. Conflict situations that have already escalated significantly are often very difficult to contain without help, and in these situations, families should not hesitate to ask for professional support.

4.1 Individual Work: Reflecting on One's Own Part

Key Phrase:
There is no way around consciousness and awareness.

An early text on conflicts in family businesses identifies "consciousness raising" as an essential part of conflict work.[1] Everyone can start to work on this themselves and can become aware of the unique and complex

---
[1] Harvey and Evans (1994).

configuration of a family business and how conflicts almost inevitably arise from this complexity. Those who learn to observe themselves can question their own tendency to count back the causes of a problem to a single person, can stop themselves imputing motives to the other person, and can reflect on whether there may be other possible narratives of a situation.

Those who observe themselves, will change." This saying contains much truth. Those who reflect on their own outrage and indignation are no longer quite so much at its mercy: "What is the logic of my notion of justice? Where does it come from? Can I put my logic aside in the face of the other person's? Can I get involved in understanding their logic?" Remember that understanding their logic does not have to mean agreeing with it.

It is not easy to observe the conflict system from the outside if you are severely affected yourself. Particularly when the situation has escalated, both sides have already caused considerable damage; each has taken its revenge and, in the process, shattered relationships and weakened connections. The point here is not to excuse such actions—often enough, the pent-up resentment on the other side is the biggest obstacle when it comes to reconciliation—but to see them as stages of escalation. You can map out the conflict and then turn the page 180 degrees—what does it look like from the other side?

4.2 Distinction: Interests and Positions

> **Key Phrase:**
> Question your own position and that of others: "Why is this important to you?"

In conflict situations, the parties have often settled on an immutable position:

- "As long as he doesn't let go, there's no point in talking to each other at all."—"If my daughter starts like this, we might as well forget it."

- "If I don't get at least x-thousand euros, there won't be an end to it."—"You won't get a penny, that's for sure."
- "Before we even start talking, he has to apologise to me."—"That's ridiculous! If anyone should apologise, it's her."

Experience shows that agreement often is impossible (or much harder) at the level of positions because, by committing to a position, a "win-lose" context is created: every deviation from this position, every compromise, is associated with a loss of face, because of the original commitment not to budge an inch.

Therefore, professional conflict counselling will often first attempt to discover the *interests* behind the rigid and factually presented positions in individual discussions. Interests are the "silent motives behind the confusion of positions"[2] and have to do with concerns, wishes, hopes, and, first of all, emotions. At this level, if it is possible to enter into a mode of mutual understanding, it is not uncommon to find a solution that satisfies both sides. However, it will not always be as simple as in the often cited children's quarrel over the orange, where the parents discover that one wants to grate the peel to make a cake and the other's interest simply lies in drinking the juice.

The question which usually is asked first (and that you can ask yourself) is "Why is it so important to me? What do I want to ensure?" These personal interests are generally concerned with basic human needs: security, economic livelihood, a sense of belonging, recognition, respect, and self-determination.

Thus, in the first position outlined above, we can imagine that the daughter's perspective is focused on a desire not to have to work under and answer to her father forever; she wants the chance to develop herself and her self-esteem in running the business. For the father, it may be especially important to be able to decide for himself when and how he "lets go" and how his economic livelihood can be guaranteed afterwards. We can imagine that it is easier to talk about these issues—as long as each is willing to listen to the other—than to face "either-or" demands (which may be expressed in anger).

---

[2] Fisher et al. (2011).

The development of a *questioning heuristic* within the business family, when dissent arises, could be the first step towards achieving conflict resolution competence within the family or, at least, among the "welfare officers" or members of the family committee responsible for family peace. In this way, the hardening of interests and positions can be prevented at an early stage.

4.3 Breaking Out of the Vicious Cycle I: Slow Down

An essential moment in searching for de-escalation in oneself is the introduction of an element of change. The first element is *deceleration*. Conflict dynamics are characterised by a high intensity, the belief that "if we don't hit back right now, they think they can get away with it." This attitude simply shows how far one party is already stuck in the trap of the mechanisms described above and already turning the escalation screw. Immediate, indignant retaliation only encourages the other party to react in the same way. Sometimes even doing nothing is the better alternative: "Strike while the iron is cold".[3] Interrupting an escalating situation in a friendly way involves no loss of face. The argument can be postponed and continued when one's own indignation has abated.

4.4 Breaking Out of the Vicious Circle II: Gestures, the Magic Word "Partially", and "Small Credit Offers"

Key Phrase:
Friendly gestures are the best antidote to the hostile perception error.

---

[3] Alon and Omer (2006).

Experience shows that good relationships are characterised by a high number of "good moments". Couples therapy, for example, uses the 5:1 ratio, that is, one negative interaction needs at least five positive ones to be reversed.[4] These are usually small actions: a friendly smile, a cheerful "good morning". If a conflicted relationship has become bogged down, even such small things are not easy—why say a friendly greeting to someone who is giving you a nasty look, especially if it is likely to be countered with "Leave me alone"?

Here, it is helpful to recall the explanations of the hostile attributional error given earlier. In a conflict system, a friendly gesture is often initially interpreted negatively, as a trick, "Is he trying to mock me now with his stupid grin?" and commented on accordingly. It is therefore very important to react calmly to any rejection or provocation and, if possible, not comment further on it but remain friendly on the next occasion. A significant opportunity to break out of the vicious circle is created by reacting to a provocation, not with hostility (as anticipated by the opponent) but with a kind or at least neutral response—contrary to all expectations! Small gestures like this, made unconditionally, increase the chances of undermining the hostile perceptual error, although, of course, they are not guaranteed to do so.[5]

For example, we lose nothing by partially agreeing with the other person: "I have thought about last night's argument, and just wanted to tell you that I do partly agree with you. We don't have to go into it now, I just wanted to tell you." "Partially" is a very special, a de-demonising word, which can create space between "either" and "or".

The following "Small Offers of Credit"[6] exercise follows this thinking. In most cases, it will require the facilitation of a third person; at a less escalated stage, it may also be possible first to answer the questions separately and then to discuss them together. Essentially, it is about limited offers of trust, each giving the other a chance. It may even be possible to work through them alone, acting without the other person knowing your intention. The exercise consists of the following steps:

---

[4] Gottman (1994).
[5] Omer and von Schlippe (2023).
[6] Further elaborated by the authors on an idea from Glasl (2013).

- What could you do in, let's say, the next 2 weeks to improve the atmosphere (e.g. show or avoid certain behaviours for a fortnight)? Important here: we're talking about small signs, not "giving the big and public excuse for everything" but rather refraining from sarcastic comments on whatever the other one says or does.
- What could you suggest to the other party that would be a "small offer of credit" (something that they could do or refrain to do for a defined period)? What kind of behaviour/communication/symbolic action would be a sign of a small degree of confidence?
- What other small "credit offers" could in return you make yourself to the other party?
- How can you communicate these in a way that minimises the risk of misunderstanding?
- For which of your "credit offers" could you waive guarantees during this period as long as there is an agreement to meet at the end of the period to review it?

4.5 Breaking Out of the Vicious Cycle III: Make Yourself Unpredictable

Key Phrase:
If it doesn't work, try something else!

One paradoxical characteristic of conflict systems is that the reactions of the parties involved are almost entirely predictable. An insult is followed by a counter-insult, a demand by rejection, and a conciliatory gesture by scornful laughter. When the conflict dynamics have taken on a life of their own, the parties simply follow the choreography set by the conflict and they do this—as mentioned earlier—without being aware of having already entered the carousel of indignation and outrage. Rather, each one still believes that they can completely control themselves, even when they have already lost the ability to act independently: "After all, there was no alternative, I had to act this way" (incidentally, this is how wars usually start): "People often overlook the fact that they are in a conflict spiral and view themselves as responding to persistent annoyance from Other".[7] With each provocation, to which the other reacts—predictably—with a further stage of escalation, the expectation structures of the conflict system are consolidated and the demonic descriptions deepen: 'He's really a bad person!'

Here, it can be useful to use the classic rule of thumb: "If it doesn't work … try something else!" You can ask yourself what the expected reaction would be in this context: "What does the other person expect me to do? What would be an unexpected alternative? How could I surprise them and increase the chance of a constructive turn in events?" To avoid misunderstanding, this does not mean to always give in. On the contrary, some conflict systems are characterised by a reciprocal conditionality of demands and yielding. In these cases, it can make sense to actively—and non-violently—show resistance.[8] At this point, however, it is advisable also to seek outside help.

- One option is to remain silent (but without a hostile attitude), where you would normally react with a torrent of words. Importantly, this silence is not the same as sulking ("You'll do what you want anyway!") It is more of an underlying meditative attitude that involves a conscious inward decision not to be drawn into the dynamic. You can tell yourself something like: "The pattern now would be to respond loudly. I will resist the pull of the pattern and I'm curious to see what happens then!" Of course it needs some self-discipline to withstand the feelings of indignation and outrage. But becoming a kind of researcher ("how will the situation change if I act in an unexpected way?") may be of help here.
- "Constructive break out" can be helpful in combination with the option of remaining silent. Instead of leaving the room with a slam of the door as usual—which would be a form of "destructive break out"—you might say something like, "I don't think it would be a good idea to answer now as I might say things I'll regret. I'm not going to

---

[7] Pruitt and Kim (2004, p. 97).
[8] Omer and von Schlippe (2023) provide detailed information on ways of overcoming escalation by non-violent means.

continue the conversation now, so I'll leave for the moment but I'll come back to this later!"
- Another option is the wonderful word "partially" (see above). What would you lose if you were to reply to an attack on the part of the other side by saying something like: "When I listen to what you say, I think you may be *partially* right!" It is a small step towards reaching out to the other person, without capitulating. At the same time, it introduces a degree of differentiation to the communication: "partially" can offer several shades of meaning between black and white.

When a conflict escalates, both sides are highly predictable because the impulsive response is so easy for the other side to foresee. When looking at yourself, ask yourself what behaviour the other side would expect of you in the given situation and do something different. The important thing is not necessarily to surprise the other person but to put yourself in an experimental mode—in other words, to surprise yourself: what potential new communicative links are created when I leave my well-trodden paths?[9]

Of course, if you are upset or angry yourself, advice to break the vicious circle is easily given but hard to follow! It is difficult and will take considerable effort to act differently, but this is precisely why it is important to change the pattern you have become entangled in and take a step back from the logic of winning or losing. If we imagine conflicts as highly integrated social systems (parasites, see 3.5), one party's behaviour is heavily determined by that of the other: any provocation is countered quickly and vigorously, exactly the reaction that the original provocation sought.

---

[9] Once you grasp this idea, it can be fun to try it out in everyday life, too. The call to "Do something different" can relate to many areas of life where change can be refreshing. Which foot do you normally get out of bed on? What side of the bed do you or your partner normally sleep on? Have you ever tried swapping? Have you ever spent a night under the stars? When at the deli, why not simply try buying the same as the person in front of you instead of your usual favourites, or try a similar approach when buying a shirt? Have you ever been to a shooting match, an opera, a casino, a classical, punk, or rock concert? Have you ever taken pot luck at the theatre or cinema and bought a ticket for a film or a play you know nothing about?

4.6 Breaking Out of the Vicious Circle IV: Assuming Good Intentions

> **Key Phrase:**
> If you assume that others have good intentions, it is more likely that they will follow these good intentions.

The demonisation of the other party was described above as an essential element in the intensification of conflicts. The more an individual succeeds in de-demonising the other, the better the prospects for conflict resolution. Of course, it is taking a risk to impute good intentions to the other party—intentions are not always good! However, a "leap of faith" (in Luhmann's words) may in the long term prove to be the more farsighted strategy, providing it is not overly naive. In families, it can certainly be very helpful as an interim measure to proactively avoid making hostile perception errors yourself and assume the other person essentially has honourable intentions—and this appears to be helpful in organisations, too. Even if the other person's actions are incomprehensible, it can be useful to imagine that they are also an "affected party" and that they are coping with feelings of shame and powerlessness or feel their personal sense of justice has been offended. All this can help us see the other side in a friendlier way, although this is of course a difficult undertaking when we are engaged in conflict. Yet this "de-demonisation" is important if we are to manage the "parasite" and learn that our real opponent is the escalation itself or the shared predicament, not the other person. In a conflict, both sides are stuck in the same boat.

References

Alon, N., & Omer, H. (2006). *The psychology of demonization: Promoting acceptance and reducing conflict.* Routledge.

Fisher, R., Ury, W., & Patton, B. (2011). *Getting to yes. Negotiating agreement without giving in.* Houghton Mifflin Harcourt Publishing Company.

Glasl, F. (2013). *Konfliktmanagement: Ein Handbuch zur Diagnose und Behandlung von Konflikten für Organisationen und ihre Berater* (11. Aufl.). Haupt.

Gottman, J. M. (1994). *What predicts divorce? The relationship between marital processes and marital outcomes.* Lawrence Erlbaum.

Harvey, M., & Evans, R. E. (1994). Family business and multiple levels of conflict. *Family Business Review, 7*(4), 331–348.

Omer, H., & von Schlippe, A. (2023). *Autorität durch Beziehung. Gewaltloser Widerstand in Beratung, Therapie, Erziehung und Gemeinde* (10. vollständig überarbeitete und erweiterte Auflage). Vandenhoeck & Ruprecht.

Pruitt, D., & Kim, S. H. (2004). *Social conflict: Escalation, stalemate, and settlement* (3rd ed.). McGrawhill.

5

Dealing with Conflicts on the Collective Level: Family Strategy and More

The following section suggests approaches to addressing business family conflicts at the level of the family community. The first step is to identify the form of conflict and the forum in which it should be resolved. This section depicts typical family strategy issues addressed within the context of family strategy development in relation to dealing with conflicts. Finally, it outlines the ideal multi-stage procedure for resolving conflicts. The guide concludes by providing reflection questions to identify existing attitudes towards conflict and ways to address it in a business family.

5.1 Classification of the Conflict and the Solution Level

> **Key Phrase:**
> Not every family conflict should be taken to the shareholders' meeting; not every disagreement about an investment should cloud the next family meeting.

It is often far from easy to determine the nature of a conflict and to assign it to the relevant system. Thus, not every family conflict needs to be resolved through elaborate mediative or legal procedures. For example, in the case of a massive escalation between two family members that affects the decision-making capacity of the management or the shareholders, the conflict clauses that should be included in the rules of procedure, advisory board statutes, or shareholders' agreement must ultimately be applied, following attempts at mediation. The different causes and levels of disputes in family businesses and their judicial interpretation have already been described elsewhere; they will not be elaborated in detail here.[1]

The types of conflict or degrees of escalation shown in Fig. 5.1 allow us to make an initial classification of the type of conflict that may exist.[2] In the second step, the appropriate procedures for resolving conflicts within the family—or disputes within the circle of shareholders—must then be selected.

In principle, as a prevention measure, a business family should think through all conceivable types of conflict and check whether corresponding conflict clauses are included within legally valid contracts and articles of association, formulated to ensure the ability to continue making decisions within the business in the event of a conflict escalating.

---

[1] We would recommend here the explanations given in the WIFU practical guide on the legal handling of shareholder conflicts by Otte (2018, download on www.wifu.de) as well as works by Frohnmayer and Klein-Wiele (2014); for English, see Pieper et al. (2013), Singer (2018), Sorenson (1999), Koerner and Fitzpatrick (2006). All these publications provide a well-grounded overview of the typical causes of disputes and offer valuable advice on moderative and legal options for dispute resolution.

[2] Frohnmayer and Klein-Wiele (2014).

5 Dealing with Conflicts on the Collective Level: Family Strategy…

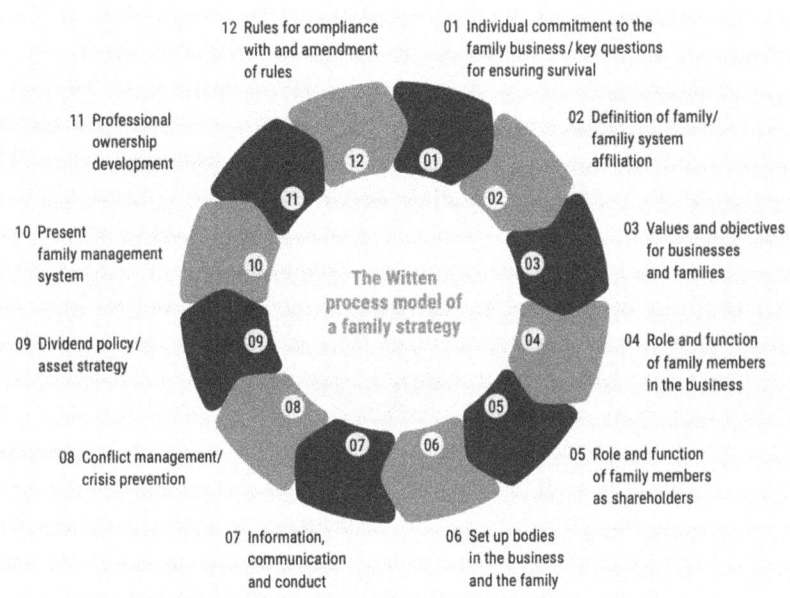

Fig. 5.1 Criteria for the selection of appropriate dispute resolution instruments (Rüsen, von Schlippe, & Groth, 2022, p. 6)

5.2 Conflict Prevention Within Family Strategy Development

> **Key Phrase:**
> The time to repair the roof is when the sun is shining: maintain the family's ability to decide.

Unless they have been scarred by conflict in the past, business families often have no conflict prevention or negotiation measures in place. The foregoing illustrates why families do not typically engage in a systematic and professional consideration of conflict. In our work with business families, we have repeatedly found that their members initially find it very difficult to conduct a dry run of the worst conceivable developments in the family circle as a means of conflict prevention. They often believe that they can control conflicts that have arisen just with a clarifying discussion within the family. Families who have already experienced conflicts that have threatened—or had the potential to threaten—their existence or have been told such stories by members of previous generations are more open to including targeted conflict prevention measures within their family governance. The *Witten Model of Family Strategy Development* developed by the authors devotes one of twelve thematic blocks to this topic area (see Fig. 5.1).[3]

Within the framework of such a process, which is usually moderated, procedures and rules define how the members of the business family want to manage conflicts between family members or within the shareholder circle. A "family stress test" can reveal existing gaps in the value structure or the rules of action and behaviour within the business family.

Taking family strategy considerations into account, the primary task is to consider how the business family would like to address conflicts, and the stages in which these should be tackled and managed by the family members themselves or, if necessary, with the support of third parties. In concrete terms, it is about defining rules of conduct on, for example, how a family member can address a situation that makes them feel hurt or angry. Behavioural rules that apply to all members of the business family can be defined to prevent an escalation of conflict situations and "uninhibited family communication". For example, the well-known "48-hour rule" (the time within which a conflict is to be disclosed to a trusted person) serves on the one hand to address the problem and, on the other, to avoid approaching the person involved in the conflict directly, thus aggravating the situation. In the end, the internal or external conflict

---

[3] See in detail Rüsen et al. (2022), von Schlippe et al. (2021).

facilitator (depending on the severity of the incident) has the task of initiating a process to resolve the issue.

Other issues that need to be raised during the family strategy process—and transferred into the corresponding contracts and legally enforceable articles of association—include the delegation of particular rights to third parties outside the family (e.g. members of the supervisory body) in case of conflict. These relate to specific decision-making rights at top management level or to the individual rights of shareholders. The aim is to ensure that the decision-making ability in the business, or among the shareholders, is maintained despite conflict within the family. In this case, the shareholders bind themselves, for the good of the business, to temporarily transfer their voting rights to third parties (e.g. non-family members of the supervisory body) to avoid impairing the future viability of the business. Equivalent considerations should be integrated into the corresponding contracts in order to ensure a comprehensive and legally binding approach.

Questions on conflict that every business family should clarify as part of the development of their family strategy include:

1. How should conflict situations be handled within the family? (Who should be allowed to, should or must contact whom, when and how in a conflict situation?)
2. What options for support from outside the family should be available or provided to resolve conflicts?
3. Should the decision-making power in issues of conflict be placed in the hands of third parties (e.g. an advisory council or mediation committee) once a certain degree of escalation has been reached? (Some families even name specific external persons as moderators here, to avoid additional conflict about whom to ask.) (Fig. 5.2)

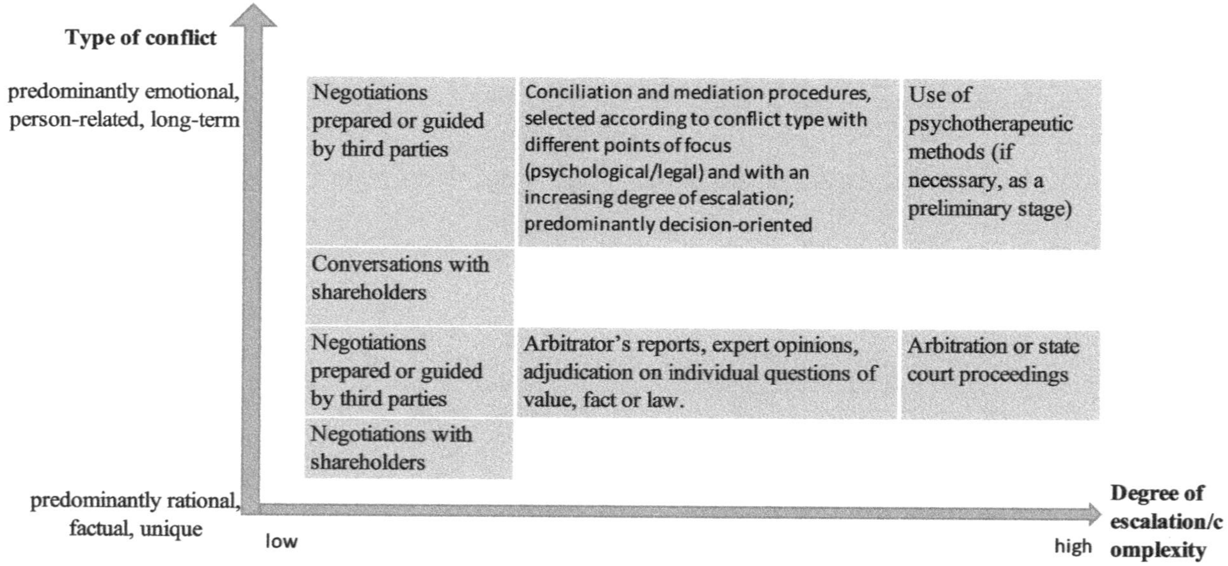

Fig. 5.2 Conflict management and crisis prevention embedded in a family strategy. Source: von Schlippe & Rüsen (2020, p. 31), translated by the authors

5.3 (Ideal) Five-Stage Procedure for Managing Conflicts

> Key Phrase:
> Don't sound the alarm straight away: clarify who should help whom, how and when.

Within the framework of a family strategy development process, concrete procedures should ideally be defined for how to address conflict within the family. It makes sense to use a standardised five-step procedure (Table 5.1).[4] The first step is to agree on the involvement of a family member who will act as a problem solver (Stage 1). This requires the existence of a family council or a dedicated person trained in conflict resolution.[5] This dedicated person attempts to achieve a resolution of the conflict through family discussions. If they are not successful, they will hand the conflict over to a defined conflict moderator from outside the family (Stage 2). An experienced expert on conflict resolution, who has been accepted by all family members at the emergence of the conflict, now addresses the conflict parties and facilitates a mediation meeting. This professional conflict moderator should ideally be identified in advance, in order to initiate conflict moderation. If the conflict moderation is unsuccessful, a mediation procedure needs to be initiated (Stage 3). The person(s) to be involved as facilitators at this stage should also be determined in advance by the business family.

If the mediation process also fails, previously appointed non-family members of the supervisory or advisory board of the business are entrusted with the development of a proposal to resolve the conflict (Stage 4).

If this approach also fails, the matter is submitted to a pre-defined arbitration tribunal for a decision (Stage 5). Here, it is important that there are clear rules to exclude legal action, so that the arbitration award can be considered legally binding.

---

[4] This framework is taken and slightly modified from Rüsen et al. (2021, p. 98.)
[5] Special training in conflict solving and communication skills should be part of every ownership competency development programme. See Rüsen (2016) and Rüsen et al. (2022).

Table 5.1 Ideal five-stage procedure for resolving conflicts (Taken and slightly modified from Rüsen, Kleve, & von Schlippe 2021, p. 98)

Step	Actors involved	Content/Activities
1	Contact person in the family committee as conflict solver in the family committee	Attempt at resolution I: Selected members of the family committee act as contact persons and try to achieve a resolution of the conflict through internal family discussions. If such attempts fail, the conflict is handed over to a conflict moderator from outside the family
2	Family external conflict moderator	Attempt at resolution II: The non-family conflict moderator undertakes conflict management. If such attempts fail, the conflict is handed over to a mediator
3	Family external mediator	Attempt at resolution III: The mediator is commissioned to conduct a mediation process. If mediation fails, an attempt at a solution is made with representatives of the supervisory body from outside the family
4	Inclusion of non-family members of the supervisory board	Attempt at resolution: Selected non-family members of the supervisory body shall endeavour to prepare a proposed solution. If this proposal is not accepted, the matter is referred to a pre-determined arbitration tribunal for a decision
5	"Third party"/ Arbitration court	Resolution by arbitration: The defined arbitration court makes a decision that is binding for all shareholders/family members by shareholder agreement (arbitration clause). The legal process is thus excluded

The effective functioning of this kind of procedure can only be ensured if the procedural steps have been clearly defined *before* a conflict arises and if the family members have already agreed on the persons to be involved. If the procedure has been made clear to all family members and agreed by them, the process should flow reasonably smoothly, due to its fixed structure and the precise definition of when each activity is carried out and by whom. This offers a strong likelihood of reducing the otherwise escalating and emotionally overloaded communications between the conflict parties (Table 5.1).

5.4 Last but Not Least: Reflective Questions on Building Conflict Skills and Conflict Management Competence Within the Business Family

> **Key Phrase:**
> Forewarned is forearmed: The "family stress test" can protect against unpleasant surprises.

The contents of this guide provide an overview of typical conflict dynamics and possible solutions for members of business families and advisers working in this context. The following reflective questions are intended to help those concerned to sharpen their own perspective on conflicts in the business family, determine the status quo, and, if necessary, take steps to prevent or manage conflicts:

- In what way and by whom should the topic of "conflict" be addressed as a structural risk within the business family?
- What is the basic attitude towards conflict in the business family? To what extent is there a taboo on discussing issues of potential conflict? (Is conflict seen as the end of the transgenerational community of trustees or as an opportunity for the further development of the people involved?)
- In what form can expectations of justice, perceptions of injustice, grievances, anger, violation of psychological contracts, or similar issues be addressed in relation to the business family? (Are intra-family "laundry days" held that enable themes to emerge in a structured form under moderation?)
- In which situations, and for which issues might it be sensible to leave a conflict as it is, not to address it or give it time to resolve itself?
- Is there an awareness within the business family of the typical conflict patterns and dynamics in family businesses (as, for example, outlined in this guide)? Are there professional ownership development programmes that include building conflict management capacity?

- Which conflicts from previous generations do family members know of? How did the family ensure that these did not escalate? How were conflicts resolved in the past (or do they remain unresolved)? Do the family members know these stories? Do they help to develop a specific conflict resilience within the business family? How far do members of later generations see themselves as separated from these stories?
- Which family member has the required trust from family members and the necessary skills (acquired through experience or training) to intervene in conflicts within the family in a de-escalating and moderating way? Which person from outside the family is sufficiently trusted to be asked for external support?
- Are conflict clauses for managing dissent included in the shareholders' agreement? Are these regularly discussed with a lawyer or revised in line with current case law?
- To what extent does the business family have a family strategy that explicitly addresses conflict management? Is there a separate chapter on managing conflicts in the respective family charter, constitution, code of conduct, or guiding principles? If not, is this an omission or a conscious decision?
- What is the planned process for resolving conflicts and how many stages does it include?

The authors associate these reflective questions with the creation of much-needed conflict awareness, in the sense of "consciousness raising".[6] If you—as interested readers—are able to use this guide in working with your own business family or your clients, our aim in writing it has been fulfilled.

References

Frohnmayer, T., & Klein-Wiele, C. (2014). *Konfliktmanagement – Methodik und Auswahl unterschiedlicher Instrumente zur Beilegung von Gesellschafterstreitigkeiten* (pp. 13–25). Familienunternehmen und Stiftungen.

---

[6] Harvey and Evans (1994).

Harvey, M., & Evans, R. E. (1994). Family business and multiple levels of conflict. *Family Business Review, 7*(4), 331–348.

Koerner, A. F., & Fitzpatrick, M. A. (2006). Family conflict communication. In J. Oetzel & S. Ting-Toomey (Eds.), *The Sage handbook of conflict communication: Integrating theory, research, and practice* (pp. 159–183). Sage.

Otte, D. (2018). *Konfliktmanagement in Familienunternehmen. Ein Praxisleitfaden zur rechtlichen Handhabung von Gesellschafterkonflikten*. WIFU-Praxisleitfaden. Witten (Germany): WIFU.

Pieper, T. M., Astrachan, J. H., & Manners, G. E. (2013). Conflict in family business: Common metaphors and suggestions for intervention. *Family Relations, 62*(3), 490–500.

Rüsen, T. A. (2016). *Krisen und Krisenmanagement in Familienunternehmen* (2. Aufl.). Springer.

Rüsen, T., Groth, T., & von Schlippe, A. (2021). 10 golden principles to guide your succession planning. *Entrepreneur & Innovation Exchange*. Retrieved May 5, 2021, from https://familybusiness.org/content/10-golden-principles-to-guide-your-succession-planning

Rüsen, T. A., Kleve, H., & von Schlippe, A. (2021). *Managing business family dynasties. Between family, organization, and network*. Springer.

Rüsen, T. A., von Schlippe, A., & Groth, T. (2022). *Family strategy development in business families – Content and forms of family governance and family management systems*. Practical guide of the Witten Institute for Family Business (WIFU). Witten (Germany): WIFU.

Singer, L. (2018). *Settling disputes: Conflict resolution in business, families, and the legal system*. Routledge.

Sorenson, R. L. (1999). Conflict management strategies used by successful family businesses. *Family Business Review, 12*(4), 325–340.

von Schlippe, A., & Rüsen, T. (2020). *Konflikte und Konfliktdynamiken in Unternehmerfamilien*. WIFU-Praxisleitfaden. WIFU.

von Schlippe, A., Rüsen, T., & Groth, T. (2021). *The two sides of the business family. Governance and strategy across generations*. Springer.

6

Wrap-Up: 18 Key Phrases

1. *Family businesses are fertile fields for conflict.*
2. *Conflict in business families should be seen as "the rule"; rather, the absence of conflict should be regarded as the exception that needs explanation.*
3. *Many conflicts in family businesses can be understood as more or less intelligent attempts to solve paradoxical dilemmas.*
4. *Attributing complexity to a single person increases escalation.*
5. *In conflict, cognitive function begins to narrow and the other person will be increasingly described in demonic terms.*
6. *When a sense of justice is violated, clear thinking stops.*
7. *At some point, "We have a conflict" becomes "The conflict has us."*
8. *It's not difficult to fall into the abyss: just go down, a bit faster, step by step—there'll be no way back!*
9. *Inherited conflicts are the hardest to resolve.*
10. *There is no way around awareness.*
11. *Question your own position and that of others: "Why is this important to you?"*
12. *Friendly gestures are the best antidote to the hostile perception error.*
13. *If it doesn't work, try something else!*

14. *If you assume that others have good intentions, it is more likely that they will follow these good intentions.*
15. *Not every family conflict should be taken to the shareholders' meeting; not every disagreement about an investment should cloud the next family meeting.*
16. *The time to repair the roof is when the sun is shining: maintain the family's ability to decide.*
17. *Don't sound the alarm straight away: clarify who should help whom, how, and when.*
18. *Forewarned is forearmed: The "family stress test" can protect against unpleasant surprises.*

Responsible for the Content

WIFU Foundation
Prof. Dr. Arist von Schlippe, Prof. Dr. Tom A. Rüsen
Alfred-Herrhausen-Strasse 48
58448 Witten
Germany

Illustrations: Björn von Schlippe, copyright held by Björn von Schlippe
Please note: Where this practical guide includes references to persons in the masculine, these apply equally to persons of any gender.

October 2023

GPSR Compliance

The European Union's (EU) General Product Safety Regulation (GPSR) is a set of rules that requires consumer products to be safe and our obligations to ensure this.

If you have any concerns about our products, you can contact us on

ProductSafety@springernature.com

In case Publisher is established outside the EU, the EU authorized representative is:

Springer Nature Customer Service Center GmbH
Europaplatz 3
69115 Heidelberg, Germany

www.ingramcontent.com/pod-product-compliance
Lightning Source LLC
LaVergne TN
LVHW041204250326
834689LV00001BA/2